A New Copernican Turn

This short book discusses the latest in terms of cosmology's knowns and unknowns and sets out to ascertain the potential of Orthodox Christian theology for accommodating the current scientific view of the universe. It also addresses one of cosmology's unknowns, the destiny of the self in the vastness of space, a topic that has caused angst since the dawn of modern science.

The book examines, accordingly, the signs of a "New Copernican Turn" within contemporary culture, favouring the self and its meaningful encounters with the infinite universe, at the forefront of which being the quest for a physics that views something akin to the self as undergirding reality, not as an inconsequential byproduct of natural phenomena. The book further shows that theological, spiritual, and religious forms of nature contemplation and wonder facilitate the self's creative intersection with the universe. It amounts to an exercise in science-engaged Orthodox theology that takes contemporary cosmology as a starting point.

The intended audience of this book is scholars and researchers of science and religion, religious studies, philosophers, and theologians.

Doru Costache is a Romanian Orthodox priest living in Australia and Associate Professor of Theology at the Sydney College of Divinity. He is the current Selby Old Fellow in Religious History of the Orthodox Christian Faith at the University of Sydney Library. Until recently, he was Honorary Research Associate in Studies in Religion, the University of Sydney's School of Humanities. He coedits ISCAST's interdisciplinary journal, *Christian Perspectives on Science and Technology*. His lecturing and research career spans almost thirty years. His latest monograph was *Humankind and the Cosmos: Early Christian Representations* (2021).

Geraint F. Lewis is Professor of Astrophysics at the Sydney Institute for Astronomy in the University of Sydney's School of Physics. He has more than three decades of experience studying the cosmos, focusing on the "dark side," the matter and energy that shape the universe around us. He is the author of more than five hundred academic publications and a populariser of science through public speaking and media presentations. He has written three popular science books on the universe's wonders, of which the latest was *Where Did the Universe Come From? And Other Cosmic Questions* (with C. Ferrie 2021).

Routledge Focus on Religion

Owning the Secular
Religious Symbols, Culture Wars, Western Fragility
Matt Sheedy

Cross-Cultural and Religious Critiques of Informed Consent
Edited by Joseph Tham, Alberto García Gómez, and Mirko Daniel Garasic

Worldview Religious Studies
Douglas J Davies

White Evangelicals and Right-Wing Populism: How Did We Get Here?
Marcia Pally

Rape Culture in the House of David: A Company of Men
Barbara Thiede

Counseling Survivors of Religious Abuse
Paula J. Swindle, Craig C. Cashwell, and Jodi L. Tangen

Conspiracy Theorizing
Analysis and Scriptural Critique
Gerald A. Arbuckle

A New Copernican Turn
Contemporary Cosmology, the Self, and Orthodox Science-Engaged Theology
Doru Costache and Geraint F. Lewis

For more information about this series, please visit: www.routledge.com/Routledge-Focus-on-Religion/book-series/RFR

A New Copernican Turn
Contemporary Cosmology, the Self, and Orthodox Science-Engaged Theology

**Doru Costache and
Geraint F. Lewis**

LONDON AND NEW YORK

First published 2025
by Routledge
4 Park Square, Milton Park, Abingdon, Oxon OX14 4RN

and by Routledge
605 Third Avenue, New York, NY 10158

Routledge is an imprint of the Taylor & Francis Group, an informa business

© 2025 Doru Costache and Geraint F. Lewis

The right of Doru Costache and Geraint F. Lewis to be identified as authors of this work has been asserted in accordance with sections 77 and 78 of the Copyright, Designs and Patents Act 1988.

All rights reserved. No part of this book may be reprinted or reproduced or utilised in any form or by any electronic, mechanical, or other means, now known or hereafter invented, including photocopying and recording, or in any information storage or retrieval system, without permission in writing from the publishers.

Trademark notice: Product or corporate names may be trademarks or registered trademarks, and are used only for identification and explanation without intent to infringe.

British Library Cataloguing-in-Publication Data
A catalogue record for this book is available from the British Library

ISBN: 978-1-032-86349-8 (hbk)
ISBN: 978-1-032-86350-4 (pbk)
ISBN: 978-1-003-52713-8 (ebk)

DOI: 10.4324/9781003527138

Typeset in Times New Roman
by Apex CoVantage, LLC

To Basarab Nicolescu, physicist, philosopher, poet.

In the memory of Fred Hoyle, cosmological maverick.
Not always correct, but when he was, it was wonderful!

Contents

List of Figures   ix
Acknowledgements   xi

1 Introduction   1

Orthodox Christianity and Science-Engaged Theology 2
Science-Engaged Orthodox Theology and Contemporary Cosmology 7
A Proleptic Synthesis of This Book 10

2 What We Know and What We Don't Know about the Universe: Scientific Perspectives   19

Historical Preliminaries 19
What Do We Know? 22
    The Universe Had a Beginning 22
    The Universe Has Evolved and Changed 23
    The Universe Is Dominated by the Dark Side 25
    The Universe Is Winding Down 26
What Don't We Know? 27
    We Don't Know Where the Universe Comes from 27
    The Dark Side Remains a Mystery 28
    We Don't Understand Why the Universe Is the Way It Is 29
    Do We Really Know Where the Universe Is Going? 31
Conclusions 32

3 What We Know and What We Don't Know about the Universe: Theological Perspectives   35

Should Orthodox Theology Be Afraid of Cosmology? 38
Cosmology and Traditional Wisdom 44
The Dark Side of Things and Divine Activity 48
Open Questions 54

4 The Self and the Universe in the Age of Science: For Another Copernican Turn   67

The Predicament of the Self 67
The Return of the Self 74
The Contemplative Self, Past and Present 80
  Patristic Ways of Contemplation 82
  Modern Orthodox Literature 87
  The Contemporary Turn to Wonder
    and Contemplation 90

5 Conclusions   103

Bibliography   *107*
Index of Names   *124*
Thematic Index   *126*

Figures

1.1a,b   Visual Integrations of Science and Theology. The left-side image (Figure 1.1a) shows a fourteenth-century Byzantine zodiacal fresco from St Michael the Archangel Monastery in Lesnovo, Republic of North Macedonia. The right-side image (Figure 1.1b) shows graph no. 15 in Ebenezer Sibly's *A new and complete illustration of the occult sciences*, two vols (London, 1792–1800). We are not interested in astrology here. We use these images as examples of ingenious integration of the theological universe and contemporary systems of the world, the zodiacal cosmos and the heliocentric one, respectively. Theology and the available scientific cosmography are distinct but not disentangled.   3

2.1   The Hubble Ultra Deep Field. Released in 2004, this image from the Hubble Space Telescope represented more than eleven days of exposure to an apparently blank piece of sky. As well as a few stars in our cosmic backyard, this image contains almost ten thousand individual galaxies, a tiny fraction of the trillion galaxies out there in the observable universe.   20

2.2   An Example of Cosmological Fine-Tuning. This considers the strength of the fine structure constant, responsible for the electromagnetic interaction, and the strong force that holds the nucleus of our atoms together. Our universe is marked as "You are here" in a sliver where the combinations of parameters allow the universe to be habitable. Other combinations result in the universe being robbed of the complexity that is essential for any form of life.   30

x *Figures*

3.1 An Early Example of Scientific Peer Review. The images show pages from the first edition of Isaac Newton's *Philosophiae naturalis principia mathematica* ("Mathematical principles of natural philosophy"; London, 1686), which include notes and corrections in preparation for the second edition. Newton had sent copies of the book to colleagues across Europe for peer review and feedback. The images show notes in the hand of John Craig, a Scottish mathematician who helped Newton, and his assistant, Roger Cotes, to organise the feedback received and to prepare the revised edition of the book.   36

3.2 Christian Aristotelian Cosmography. The image shows page 4 of Pierre Gassendi's *Institutio astronomica* ("Astronomical instruction"; London, 1653), a work where the author reviews existing astronomical theories and presents his own discoveries. The edition also includes Galileo Galilei's *Sidereus nuncius* and Johannes Kepler's *Dioptrice*, important works of telescopic astronomy. The geocentric view of the cosmos shown here served as an axiological platform for the ancient and medieval values.   40

3.3 Jesuit Astronomers and the Siamese Populace. The image shows item 26 on page 230 of Guy Tachard's *A relation of the voyage to Siam performed by six Jesuits, sent by the French King, to the Indies and China, in the year, 1685* (London, 1688). It presents in contradistinction the Jesuit astronomers equipped with lunettes and the locals frightened by a lunar eclipse.   42

4.1 A Model of Stonehenge. The image shows item 6 at page 51 of Johann Georg Keyssler's book, *Antiquitates selectae septentrionales et Celticae* (Hanover, 1790). It presents a schematic depiction of Stonehenge as an example of prehistoric symbolic cosmos, where astronomical and life rhythms are culturally immortalised.   76

4.2a,b Byzantine celestial representations. The left-side image (Figure 4.2a) shows a Byzantine image of Christ surrounded by the sun, the moon, and stars against the backdrop of saints at Hagia Sophia Church, Mystras, fourteenth century. The right-side image (Figure 4.2b) shows a seventeenth-century depiction of Christ as the centre of the visible and the invisible universe, represented by angels and the zodiacal signs, at Dekoulou Monastery in Mani. The two images exemplify the interest of Orthodox Christians in interpreting the cosmos as Christ-centred.   85

Acknowledgements

This short book was written within the framework of the project "Science and Orthodoxy around the World" ("SOW"), which ran at the Institute of Historical Research of the National Hellenic Research Foundation (Athens, 2020–2023) with the support of the Templeton World Charity Foundation, Inc. The opinions expressed in this publication are those of the authors and do not necessarily reflect the views of either the project "SOW" or the Foundation. The authors are grateful to the "SOW" colleagues who offered advice and feedback in the early stages of research: Bruce (Seraphim) Foltz, Christopher Knight, Nikolaos Livanos, Gerasimos Merianos, Efthymios Nicolaidis, and Sandy Sakorrafou.

Geraint F. Lewis conducted research at the University of Sydney's Institute for Astronomy in the School of Physics. In turn, Doru Costache worked as an honorary research associate in Studies in Religion at the University of Sydney's School of Humanities and at the Sydney College of Divinity. The authors are grateful to the University of Sydney colleagues Carole Cusack, Roland Fletcher, Iain Gardner, Christopher Hartney, Jay Johnston, and Garry Trompf for insightful conversations that helped them clarify matters pertaining to this project.

During the last several months of drafting, editing, and revising the manuscript, Costache was also the Selby Old Fellow in Religious History of the Orthodox Christian Faith at the University of Sydney Library (2023–2024). He is extremely grateful to the Trustees of the Selby Old Foundation for this opportunity, as well as to the University of Sydney Library's Philip Kent and Elizabeth Litting for their competent and friendly guidance. As the Selby Old Fellow, Costache was able to tap into the resources of the library's Rare Books and Special Collections (RBSC). He is therefore thankful to Julie Sommerfeldt and her wonderful team—Fiona Berry, Anne Goodfellow, Emily Kang, Charlotte Kowalski, and Leen Rieth—for introducing him to the universe of rare books and for helping him to trace relevant sources and illustrations. He extends due thanks to Kim Williams for digitising the RBSC images included in the first, third, and fourth chapters of this book.

The authors are also thankful to the six anonymous Routledge reviewers for their encouragement and suggestions, as well as to Lucie Bartonek, Payal Bharti, and Rebecca Clintworth for the professional and prompt advice that led to the publication of this work.

Doru Costache
Geraint F. Lewis

1 Introduction

This little book discusses the latest in terms of cosmology's knowns and unknowns and sets out to ascertain the potential of Orthodox Christian theology for accommodating the current scientific view of the universe. This focus transpires through its second and third chapters, of which one elaborates on contemporary cosmology while the other engages relevant matters from a theological perspective. The book furthermore addresses one of cosmology's unknowns, the destiny of the self in the vastness of space, a topic that has caused angst since the dawn of modern science.

The fourth chapter examines, accordingly, the signs of a "New Copernican Turn" within contemporary culture, favouring the self or, rather, undertaking to bridge the self and the universe.[1] At the forefront of this shift is the quest for a physics that considers the self, or something like it, a fundamental component of reality, not an inconsequential byproduct of natural phenomena. Against this backdrop, the fourth chapter aims to show that theological, religious, and philosophical forms of nature contemplation can bridge the ontological gap between the self and the universe, as well as the epistemological gap between anthropology and cosmology. In short, the book amounts to an exercise in science-engaged Orthodox theology that, for the purposes of comprehending reality, takes as a starting point the scientific view of the universe. On this note, we turn to our framework, science-engaged theology, but not before making three clarifications.

First, the scientific account, which serves as a starting point for this exercise, does not engage in either philosophical or theological speculation. What it does is merely crack the door for the philosophical and theological interpretation of contemporary cosmology without saying how this interpretation should unfold. Scientists will discover in Chapter Two a familiar world, therefore, despite it being aimed at philosophers and theologians interested in cosmological ideas. In turn, philosophers and theologians will find in it the clarity they seek about cosmology's current view of the universe.

Second, throughout this book science-engaged theology is viewed as methodologically different from the field of science and religion (also known as science and theology or faith and science), although their interests might intersect from time to time. As we understand it, science-engaged theology is a genuine form of theology. It does not take up the tune of science and religion, which is a field in its own right, but it remains aware of its concerns, methods, and aims. It is for this reason that, even when, here, we discuss topics that are of interest to science and religion scholars, we do so from a different angle, theological and hermeneutical, and within the context of cultural studies.

Third, our experiment with *Orthodox* science-engaged theology echoes Christopher Knight's recent point about steering away from the established approach in science and religion, that is, adopting generic religious ideas reliant on an abstract theism that is largely irrelevant to the experience of faith communities.[2] Knight brings to the fore the advantages of engaging the sciences within a defined traditional framework, such as Orthodox theology, which inaugurates new avenues for tackling matters of interest.[3] This, precisely, is what we undertake to do in terms of an Orthodox science-engaged theology that considers cosmology's knowns and unknowns, though not in isolation from broader cultural horizons.

Orthodox Christianity and Science-Engaged Theology

"What has been will be again, what has been done will be done again; there is nothing new under the sun." Thus reads Ecclesiastes,[4] capturing the idea of recurrent phenomena in history and hinting at the fact that knowing the past provides insights into the future. This ancient realisation has a surprisingly scientific ring to it and, across the aeons, proved to be very useful. It surely helped our "prehistoric" ancestors to realise certain patterns of nature, from the annual revolution of the skies above to the precession of equinoxes over the millennia, which was instrumental in organising life's rhythms.[5] Repeatability makes things predictable and testable, as it were, leading to practical applications. As with Galadriel's mirror, "things that were" foreshadow "things that are," and these, in turn, announce "things that yet may be."[6] So, things work in history. The same goes for cultural trends, including one that interests us here—the recent return of science-engaged theology, which, by all accounts, promises to become a creative alternative to the area variously known as science and religion, faith and science, or science and theology.

We speak of "return" given that this *theological* way of engaging the sciences, which scholars describe in various ways,[7] echoes approaches established centuries ago. Many early Christian and medieval thinkers, including Byzantine ones, were trailblazers of this trend.[8] They engaged the available "natural philosophy" of the ancients, as science was then known, primarily for apologetic and pastoral purposes but also out of genuine interest in nature's workings. What they tackled could not match, of course, the scientific culture of our days—with its deeper insight into reality and its challenging new questions—but their achievements are no less important, methodologically speaking. In short, and as we discuss in this little book, the noteworthy outcome of their efforts was a theological interpretation of nature as described by the available sciences. That those sciences are long out of date is of no consequence here. But here are a few classical examples.

In the fourth century, Basil of Caesarea and Gregory of Nyssa adopted an approach that anticipates modern science-engaged theology. Basil was critical of the inconsistencies of Hellenistic natural philosophers,[9] it is true, but he referred to Ptolemaic cosmography as a cultural given, redrafting the doctrine of creation in the language of the Alexandrian system of the world, of concentric spheres.[10] Awareness of the changing ideas of ancient scientists made him prudent about deciding on the number of Ptolemy's celestial layers. He mentioned three to seven and, more importantly, did so in order to render his theological discourse intelligible to the audiences.[11] Even where he openly criticised the natural philosophers, it was from a theological vantage point, not on scientific grounds. What he reproached to them was the fact of hypothesising about nature and the universe in utter ignorance of divine agency, which he identified as the source of their confusion.[12] His task, in turn, was to interpret the available information through the lens of theology. His approach set a very influential methodological precedent, obvious in Byzantine zodiacal iconography, and which guided scientists and theologians down to the modern era. It had a broad cultural impact even in the wake of the Copernican Turn, when Ptolemy's cosmos began to fade away (see Figure 1.1).

Figure 1.1a,b Visual Integrations of Science and Theology. The left-side image (Figure 1.1a) shows a fourteenth-century Byzantine zodiacal fresco from St Michael the Archangel Monastery in Lesnovo, Republic of North Macedonia.[13] The right-side image (Figure 1.1b) shows graph no. 15 in Ebenezer Sibly's *A new and complete illustration of the occult sciences*, two vols (London, 1792–1800).[14] We are not interested in astrology here. We use these images as examples of ingenious integration of the theological universe and contemporary systems of the world, the zodiacal cosmos and the heliocentric one, respectively. Theology and the available scientific cosmography are distinct but not disentangled.

4 *Introduction*

Gregory followed suit, showing even more interest in the natural sciences. At some point, while supposedly interpreting the Genesis narrative of creation, he referred to fire—a fundamental element of ancient physics—as the natural content of what the scriptural account calls "light."[15] Fire is not mentioned in that narrative, but Gregory was of the view that a sound representation of reality should include it for the purpose of establishing the truth about God's creation. He described, at great lengths, furthermore, the cycles of water in nature, claiming that without hydrological and meteorological information diligent readers cannot understand the proper message of Genesis regarding the world.[16] And while his meticulous description of water cycles, as much as other aspects of the natural sciences, might puzzle the pious reader, Gregory's approach is significant for at least three reasons. First, it points back to him as a saintly theologian of magnitude who was keenly interested in natural philosophy. Second, related, it shows that theological and scientific enquiries do not cancel each other and that, in fact, they complement each other as intellectual endeavours to depict reality from various vantage points. Third, following from the previous one, it showcases Gregory's exploration of cosmic rhythms as denoting God's power and wisdom.[17]

Basil and Gregory were not the first Christian theologians to show appreciation for the sciences of the ancients. Nor were they the first to engage scientific ideas theologically for the purposes of articulating their message intelligibly after the cultural parameters of their time. In the second century, for example, Clement of Alexandria praised scientifically obtained knowledge and depicted Abraham and Moses as representing a complex mindset that held together theology and science by interpreting the available information theologically.[18] The same goes for later authors, such as John of Damascus, in the eighth century, who wrote a treatise on logic, instructing the readers in the ways of correct thinking, and then introduced the Christian theological worldview by summarising the then-current scientific theories.[19] In short, before and after Basil and Gregory, these and many other patristic authors engaged the scientific knowledge available to them, such as the Ptolemaic system of the world, not the threefold cosmos of scriptural lore, to give an example relevant here.[20]

Their theological efforts paved the way for similar undertakings closer to our time, in spite of the wide historical gap from the end of the Byzantine era to the modern age. Specifically, and largely unacknowledged as contributors to this area, Orthodox representatives of the twentieth-century "neopatristic" movement—among whom noteworthy are Vladimir Lossky, Panayiotis Nellas, and Dumitru Stăniloae—tested the traditional approach against the backdrop of various modern sciences.[21] They did so tentatively, hence the widespread ignorance in regard to their relevant contributions, but their prudence is understandable. It could not have been easy—after centuries of stagnation in the Orthodox world after the Byzantine era—to retrieve the traditional method of scientific engagement and to deploy it within the framework of a very different scientific culture and against the backdrop of endless culture wars.²² Either way, their undertakings are integral to the road that led to contemporary science-engaged theology.

For example, Lossky affirmed the independence of the Christian theological worldview from any scientific description of reality but suggested that, emulating the patristic engagement of ancient cosmology, modern theologians should take into consideration their own cultural context in order to communicate cogently with their interlocutors. Apart from timid allusions, however, Lossky did not exemplify the workings of Orthodox science-engaged theology in modern times.²³ In turn, Stăniloae reformulated the traditional doctrine of creation in conversation with contemporary physics and cosmology, while Nellas developed theological anthropology in the parameters of evolutionary science.²⁴ As we shall return to Lossky and Stăniloae, here we give only the highlights of Nellas' views, whose method matches theirs but whose object—anthropology—is not immediately relevant to this work. This example will give us, however, an idea of how neopatristic theologians engaged the scientific culture of their time.

In a book that has become a classic of modern Orthodox theology,²⁵ alongside reviewing traditional sources—biblical, liturgical, and patristic—Nellas showed commitment to bridging theological and scientific anthropology. His intentions hide in plain sight in the original title of his work, Ζῶον θεούμενον, "deified animal," where the first term signifies humankind's biological side while the second one points to spiritual transformation. The association is telling.

This little-noticed interest of Nellas took the form of a courageous reassessment of traditional antecedents based on the contextual, or cultural, dimension of many patristic views of human nature. Against this backdrop, echoing Lossky's approach, he emphasised that the early Christian and Byzantine theologians engaged with the philosophy of their time, natural and otherwise. What made this engagement possible was the complex understanding that theological anthropology transcends disciplinary explorations of human nature and, related, that the human mystery is irreducible to any one definition, whether theological or other. His favourite illustration of this understanding is the comparison between an icon, a sacred representation of holy persons, and people. The way an icon can be variously perceived—as a physical object, it can be analysed chemically or artistically, while as a religious item, it lends itself to theological interpretation—so too can a human being. Specifically, grasping human nature requires scientific expertise, whereas to evaluate the human being as a *person*, taken to mean a reality of a different order, is the province of theology.²⁶ This led him to the conviction that, in its complexity, the human phenomenon requires multidisciplinary decoding. No wonder he proceeded, first, to translate theological anthropology into the contemporary vocabulary of evolutionary biology and psychology and second, to interpret this information in the light of the centre of theological anthropology, the "being-in-the-image."[27] These elements correspond to Lossky's method but are rendered anthropologically.

With these modern theologians and their colleagues in the neopatristic movement, forgotten skills and approaches began to be retrieved. A question must be asked at this juncture: Is it important to retrieve the forgotten skills of engaging the sciences theologically? Is science-engaged theology relevant to Orthodox Christianity in our day and age?

We propose that it is, for various reasons. One reason is that engaging the sciences theologically is of the essence for communicating the message of theology effectively to believers and unbelievers interested in it. Anecdotal evidence shows that most contemporary people are aware of the major scientific ideas of our time, such as the vast complexity of the spacetime continuum, that is, the universe in expansion since billions of years ago, to give one example of relevance here. Indirectly, this awareness transpires through the opposition—to this and other scientific ideas—mounted by internet "apologists" who "defend the ancient faith" against the "blasphemies of science." We will say a few more things about this group in Chapter Three. Either way, awareness of the most important scientific ideas of our time, including a smattering of cosmological information, is to be expected from most people who undergo, or who went through, secular education in the Western world. Contemporary audiences cannot be impressed by theological discourses that refer to a flat Earth or a universe created out of the blue seven millennia ago or a cosmos that can be travelled from one end to the other, on horseback, within the span of several weeks.[28]

Another reason for encouraging the theological assessment of contemporary scientific culture is the fact that it circumvents the contentiousness overall associated with science and religion—from the suspicion of disciplinary transgression about the researchers of this field to the skirmishes between militant theists and atheists this academic field aims to reconcile.[29] By interpreting scientific data through its methodological lens, hermeneutically, science-engaged theology is not affected by these difficulties. It does not need either to contest or to confirm the sciences. In turn, it facilitates the critical assimilation of scientific information within faith communities and, in turn, forwards its discourse in ways that might elicit the interest of the scientists who work free of ideological bias or who explore holistic views of reality. That said, science-engaged theology is not the only attempt at avoiding the problems usually associated with science and religion. Steps are being taken to leave behind both the suspicion and the conflict idea that linger in some quarters, despite the maturity the field has attained in the last seventy years or so.[30] The attempts alluded to here indicate a change in the wind.

Against this backdrop, while at first glance, science-engaged theology is sometimes confused with science and religion, it functions differently. It does not mean to become a field of expertise in its own right, as science and religion did, remaining essentially theological in terms of its framework, approach, and goals. But it is not theology of the usual sort either, at least not of the systematic, or dogmatic, kind. It rather aligns with the current interdisciplinary trend in religious studies, straddling diverse disciplines.[31] And it has a clear hermeneutical foundation, resembling the philosophy of science,[32] or what Andrew Davison calls "thinking with science" or "to think about what science thinks about."[33]

To be more specific, its distinctiveness within the modern theological landscape derives from the fact of considering—alongside Scripture, tradition, reason, and experience, to refer to known Wesleyan categories—scientific data and theories.[34] This does not alter either its nature or its objectives. After all, as Carmody Grey notes, throughout history, the Christian theological discourse and, more broadly, humankind's religious experience has consistently incorporated scientific assumptions.[35] Already John Henry Newman referred to this phenomenon as the "bearing of other branches of knowledge on theology."[36] But this is not all there is to it. Certain theological ideas, in turn, have been absorbed by the sciences and continue to function as axioms of the scientific method.[37] The phenomenon is ongoing, with Lisa Sideris recently showing that the Anthropocene idea is "beholden to older philosophical trends, some of which bear the imprint of theological commitments, or blur the lines between the religious and the secular."[38] This imprint comes to light, for example, in "quasi-religious conceptions of the Earth and humanity's role within it."[39] Newman called this aspect of the exchange "bearing of theology on other branches of knowledge."[40]

The nexus between science and theology is, therefore, present within the infrastructure of both worlds. It is for this reason that, as John Perry and Joanna Leidenhag have it, "scientific findings, no less than doctrinal expression, both presume and require interpretation."[41] And this, once again, is the task of science-engaged theology, namely, to interpret scientific ideas, as Christian thinkers did from at least Clement of Alexandria in the second century, if not from the New Testament authors,[42] for many centuries. To that end, taking their cue from their patristic and neopatristic predecessors, contemporary theologians will have to reappropriate forgotten skills, including the ancient philosophical discipline of nature contemplation and, together with these skills, an appreciation for scientific enquiry.

Science-Engaged Orthodox Theology and Contemporary Cosmology

This book exemplifies for Orthodox Christian theologians and other interested readers the way this goal can be achieved by addressing matters of contemporary cosmology through an interpretative exercise.

Our choice of topic—knowns and unknowns about the universe and humankind's place within it—relates to the expertise of Geraint Lewis, a professional astrophysicist with an atheistic view of the cosmos, and Doru

Costache's interest in early Christian, Byzantine, and contemporary Orthodox representations of reality. Specifically, Lewis supplies a rigorous but accessible account of contemporary cosmology, setting the record straight in regard to the victories and uncertainties of science. His contribution, the second chapter of this book, gestures friendly to readers who do not have a background in the natural sciences. In turn, Costache, an Orthodox Christian priest and a professional theologian, engages aspects of Lewis' scientific account in the other two chapters. Thus, while the second chapter equips theologians with the basics of contemporary cosmology, the third one proposes ways of interpreting this information theologically. What the third chapter undertakes is to test the capacity of Orthodox theology to accommodate up-to-date cosmological information. It does so by drawing on ancient, medieval, and modern examples. As to the fourth chapter, it engages Lewis' concluding notes about one of cosmology's unknowns, that is, the destiny of the self in the universe's far future. Here, Orthodox theology converses with the broader context of modern culture.

The approach sketched just above replicates within the parameters of contemporary culture what many early Christian and medieval thinkers did long ago, followed by the neopatristic scholars, that is, engaging scientific ideas *theologically* without needing to become scientists. We hope that this exercise will help contemporary Orthodox theologians to remember that their predecessors tackled the sciences, including cosmological information, and their manner of so doing.[43] Of course, as the Ecclesiastes teaches, we do not claim to set the skies ablaze with an unprecedented undertaking.[44] Steps towards retrieving this forgotten legacy have already been taken, though not together with a sense of the difference between science-engaged theology and the field of science and religion. This, precisely, is the reason why a robust discussion through the lens of science-engaged theology is in order.

A significant Orthodox theologian of the last century, Dumitru Stăniloae, called upon his colleagues to overcome scientific apathy and to boldly formulate "a theology of the world" that "reconciles the cosmic vision of the Fathers with a vision which grows out . . . of the natural sciences."[45] Related, he pointed out the need for a "theology of movement" or a "theological explanation" of the universe in expansion.[46] It is clear that Stăniloae was thinking of science-engaged theology already in the 1970s when he wrote his monumental synthesis of theology. To date, most Orthodox theologians have been ignoring his call.[47]

So far, no wonder, the aptitude of Orthodox theology for engaging contemporary cosmology has not been seriously tested. Stăniloae's work provides precious insights into the usefulness of quantum physics, the universe's expansion, anthropic cosmology, and evolutionary science for articulating the Orthodox worldview[48] but falls short of tackling things upfront and in a consistent way. True, here and there, he made the point—as he does in the prologue to his synthesis of dogmatic theology—about the need to replicate patristic patterns of thought within our own circumstances.[49] But, for some reason, he never spelled out the method he followed, preferring to incorporate scientific information into his theological discourse as an unproblematic cultural given. This strategy might derive from his patristic commitments; what he found in the sources was largely what he did throughout his writings; that is, refer casually to influential scientific ideas of the time. An exception from this patristic strategy makes Clement of Alexandria's decidedly methodological approach,[50] of which Stăniloae was unaware or in which, perhaps, he was not interested. Another factor that could have shaped his way of tackling scientific ideas is the fact that, throughout history, Orthodox Christianity considered reasoning and research integral to the pursuit of the truth. The sources referred to earlier prove it. Thus, Stăniloae's casual references to scientific ideas indicate a sense of normality that only readers habituated to the conflict narrative between science and religion could find intriguing and in need of methodological clarification.

A different case is Alexei Nesteruk's, whose earlier work considered methods of articulating the Orthodox worldview against the contemporary scientific backdrop.[51] His contributions from the position of a thinker equipped philosophically, scientifically, and theologically remain invaluable from the viewpoint of retrieving *today* the traditional modes of engaging science. But Nesteruk has recently taken a step back from cosmological topics. His latest writings no longer attempt to bridge Orthodox theology and cosmology, asserting that these methodologically incommensurable views of reality cannot intersect, let alone partner. In exchange, Nesteruk proposes phenomenology, hermeneutics, and cultural—or rather theological—anthropology as topics for conversation.[52] What prompted this turn is primarily the realisation of what he takes for an irreducible tension between anthropology and cosmology, epistemologically speaking, and between humankind and the cosmos, ontologically speaking.[53] His recent proposal could, of course, elicit the interest of philosophers and theologians but excludes both cosmologists from the conversation and cosmology from the scope of contemporary Orthodox thinking. Stăniloae's "theology of the world" remains a desideratum. Throughout the present book, Nesteruk's supposedly irreconcilable tension appears under the guise of the self's predicament of feeling "lost in the cosmos" and is the problem to solve, not a solution.

We have to ask, therefore, whether Orthodox theology can be as scientifically committed today as it has been in the past. Can it tackle cosmological matters cogently? This little book suggests that it can, on both counts. More precisely, by setting up the exercise mentioned above, it endeavours to show that the Orthodox representation of reality can rebuild itself by engaging contemporary cosmology. After all, it did so many times in the past when it tackled Aristotelianism, Platonism, Ptolemaic cosmography, Stoicism, and other worldviews. To our knowledge, the present book is among the first undertakings to discuss matters from the viewpoint of *Orthodox* science-engaged theology and the first one to tackle cosmology and Orthodox theology through the lens of science-engaged theology.

Before we proceed, a summary of our discourse is in order, to clarify the parameters of the exercise in Orthodox science-engaged theology proposed here.

A Proleptic Synthesis of This Book

The book focuses on three major themes. First, it considers the complexity of contemporary cosmology, which, together with its fascinating discoveries, acknowledges the existence of a vast amount of unknowns about the universe. Awareness of the unknown discourages the triumphalist narrative of previous decades when scientists and the public alike applauded the near end of all scientific quests.[54] In turn, this awareness challenges scientists to continue the exploration of the universe, even at the cost of having to agree that a new physics is needed instead of the current one. Very possibly, the physics of the future might cross into areas currently considered off-limits for science. The signs of this shift are not entirely absent.[55]

Second, the book proposes that Orthodox Christian theology—with its traditional interest in making sense of reality at the nexus of various disciplines—can accommodate contemporary cosmology, with its many knowns and unknowns, and that some of its intuitions, in turn, are compatible with the scientific culture of our age, including the current quest for a new physics. Among these intuitions are noteworthy, for example, the understanding of divine activity as occurring in the universe's infrastructure on an ongoing basis; the view of reality as a synergetic event of dynamic evolution; a rich concept of nature that transcends the known binaries of matter and spirit or natural and supernatural; the fact of considering reality in eschatological perspective, with signs of the shape of things to come being already accessible via mystical experiences and noetic perceptions.

Third, against one of the unknowns of contemporary cosmology—namely, the status and the destiny of the self in the universe—and the view that cosmology necessarily excludes the self from the ultimate algorithm of reality, this book undertakes to show that the current quest for a new physics, combined with modern iterations of philosophical, religious, and theological disciplines such as nature contemplation, can lead to a New Copernican Turn. This turn, amounting to the acceptance of the self as a fundamental ingredient of nature, can provide our culture with new insights into the nature of the universe and bring with it a sense of meaningfulness for scientists and nonscientists alike. It can also help bypass what we further down call a "resigned attitude," that is, the view that our problem is the self and that it should be altogether abandoned for the sake of indistinctness.[56]

Methodologically speaking, the three themes, which mirror the three main chapters of the book, require different approaches. Chapter Two, for example, reviews the state of things in contemporary cosmology. It begins by sketching the history of modern cosmology from its early theorisations to the multiverse and then introduces the current view of the universe, with its knowns and unknowns. It explains what we know about the beginning and the possible end of the universe, going through cosmic evolution and the "dark side" of things (Lewis' metaphor for what cosmologists call dark matter and dark energy). It continues the consideration of the "dark side" by showing that its tantalising evidence leads scientists to embrace humility in regard to the cosmos but also spurs their desire to understand it better—an attitude that could inspire many contemporaries tortured by the perspective of a pointless existence. Yet unanswered are questions about where the universe comes from, why it is as it is, and where it is heading in the distant future. This chapter concludes with thoughts about humanity's destiny in the cosmos and the universe's own place in the grand schema of things—against the backdrop of the quest for a new physics, including the Theory of Everything, which hopefully will reveal more about reality. The exposition is on purpose clear and rigorous, befitting the scientific discourse, and while it is matter-of-fact, it is also poetically charged, in the best tradition of contemporary scientific outreach literature. The main cosmological concepts and ideas—dark energy, dark matter, gravitational waves, relativity, quantum physics, etc.—are explained for the benefit of educated nonscientists, including philosophers, scholars of religious studies, and theologians.

The third and the fourth chapters, in turn, engage the previously mentioned cosmological narrative at the crossing of the history of mentalities, philosophy, religious studies, and Orthodox Christian theology. As such, they constitute an exercise in science-engaged theology, on the one hand showing that Orthodox theology can accommodate cosmology's knowns and unknowns, on the other hand suggesting ways of using scientific information for the purposes of deepening theology's view of reality and of affirming the significance of the self within the world.

More specifically, Chapter Three considers aspects of the Orthodox worldview, primarily through the lens of its early Christian and medieval sources. It showcases, furthermore, several modern Orthodox undertakings. It emphasises the fact that, diachronically perceived, the Orthodox representation of reality displays an intriguing capacity for assimilating cosmological ideas. Interestingly, while this process of assimilation has always required the effort to rephrase theological tenets, their integrity was never affected on a fundamental level. This chapter mirrors the previous one, detailing theology's knowns and unknowns about the universe. It also highlights little-known matters such as Orthodox theology's acknowledgment of cosmic movement and evolution, its complex concept of nature, and its fondness for narratives of everything. These match important aspects pertaining to contemporary cosmology. It is this compatibility that facilitates the direct conversation between Orthodox theologians and contemporary cosmologists.

The last part of this book, Chapter Four, takes exception to the widespread view that cosmology makes no allowance for consciousness and that it condemns the self to anxiety and desperation by having people feel, as Tolkien would have it, "strangers where all other things were at home."[57] Drawing upon diverse perspectives, including Orthodox Christian wisdom in conversation with other wisdom traditions, this chapter endeavours to prove otherwise. After it maps the modern history of the human psyche terrified by the infinite universe, it proposes ways of rescuing the self from its predicament by embracing scientific cosmology—primarily the views of scientists and thinkers who consider consciousness integral to the cosmic algorithm—and by cultivating traditional disciplines such as the contemplation of nature. Thus, even though the current and future sciences might not be able to determine the cosmic significance of humankind, the self can find meaning by cultivating complex ways of perceiving reality through various disciplinary lenses. In this chapter, Orthodox theology communicates its message through many voices—ancient, medieval, and modern—and engages ideas from outside its customary purview. The discourse of these two chapters is explanatory and hermeneutical, avoiding unnecessary theological jargon.

The overarching perspective, which gives consistency to these three chapters and to the approaches deployed therein, is the framework of science-engaged theology, earlier discussed. We hope that our exercise will prove that Orthodox theology is traditionally inclined to engage the sciences and that it is equipped for tackling contemporary cosmology, even when the description of the latter comes from the plume of atheist researchers. We also hope to show that, in the process of engaging contemporary cosmology, theology reaches further clarity itself and can inspire, in turn, new avenues of thought for scientists and the public alike. Such is the case with what we call here the New Copernican Turn, which bridges the universe and the self. In this vein, anticipating one of our conclusions, for example, Orthodox theologians might discover that the different quests of Stăniloae and Nesteruk hold together; they are not irreconcilable viewpoints on reality.

Notes

1 As we see it, and to clarify the metaphor of a New Copernican Turn, this paradigm shift is as radical as Copernicus' bold heliocentric proposition in the early work *Commentariolus*, not in the way his later writing, *De revolutionibus*, conversed with Ptolemy's ancient cosmography. For a recent study of this difference, see Alberto Bardi, "The Archimedean Revolution of Nicolaus Copernicus," *Transversal: International Journal for the Historiography of Science* 14 (2023): 1–11, https://doi.org/10.24117/2526-2270.2022.i14.09.
2 Christopher C. Knight, *Eastern Orthodoxy and the Science-Theology Dialogue*, Cambridge Elements: Elements of Christianity and Science (Cambridge: Cambridge University Press, 2022), 1–3, 63. See also

Costache's review of this book in *Christian Perspectives on Science and Technology*, New Series, 3 (2024), https://doi.org/10.58913/ZMCJ1640. For the importance of adopting a view from within the religious phenomenon, broadly speaking, rather than the external and supposedly objective angle of abstract or secularised, perspectives, see Paul Tyson, "Learned Ignorance? On Enlightened Blindness to the Divine and the Demonic," *Christian Perspectives on Science and Technology*, New Series, 3 (2024): 1–26, https://doi.org/10.58913/YWEV1287.
3 Knight, *Eastern Orthodoxy*, 7, 62.
4 Ecclesiastes 1:9 (New International Version).
5 Clive Ruggles, *Ancient Astronomy: An Encyclopedia of Cosmologies and Myth* (Santa Barbara, CA: ABC Clio, 2005), 345–47; Terry MacKinnell, *The Dawning: Shedding New Light on the Astrological Ages* (Xlibris, 2011), 77–97.
6 J. R. R. Tolkien, *The Lord of the Rings*, 15th anniversary ed. (HarperCollins, 2004), 362.
7 Andrew Davison, "Science and Specificity: Interdisciplinary Teaching between Theology, Religion, and the Natural Sciences," *Zygon* 57, no. 1 (2022): 233–43; John Perry and Joanna Leidenhag, *Science-Engaged Theology*, Cambridge Elements: Elements of Christianity and Science (Cambridge: Cambridge University Press, 2023); John Perry and Joanna Leidenhag, "What Is Science-Engaged Theology?" *Modern Theology* 37, no. 2 (2021): 245–53.
8 See Doru Costache, *Humankind and the Cosmos: Early Christian Representations*, Supplements to Vigiliae Christianae 170 (Leiden and Boston, MA: Brill, 2021), 52–58, 120–35, 161–67, 223–41, 292–97, 309–26; Doru Costache, "Strange Bedfellows? Orthodox Perspectives on Theology, Spirituality, Science, and Technology," *Studia Universitatis Babes-Bolyai Theologia Orthodoxa* 65, no. 2 (2020): 5–25, esp. 12–19; Doru Costache, "Byzantine and Modern Orthodox Gnosis: From the Eleventh to the Twenty-First Century," in *The Gnostic World*, ed. Garry W. Trompf, Gunner B. Mikkelsen, and Jay Johnston, Routledge Worlds (London and New York: Routledge, 2019), 426–35; Bruce V. Foltz, *The Noetics of Nature: Environmental Philosophy and the Holy Beauty of the Visible* (New York: Fordham University Press, 2014); Wayne Hankey, "Natural Theology in the Patristic Period," in *The Oxford Handbook of Natural Theology*, ed. Russell Re Manning (Oxford: Oxford University Press, 2013), 38–56; Richard de Grijs and Doru Costache, "The Cosmology of David Bohm: Scientific and Theological Significance," *Theology and Science* 22, no. 1 (2023): 204–20, https://doi.org/10.1080/14746700.2023.2294529; Peter Harrison, "A Historian's Perspective on Science-Engaged Theology," *Modern Theology* 37, no. 2 (2021): 476–82; Oskari Juurikkala, "The Book of Nature in Patristic and Medieval Theology," *Interdisciplinary Documentation on Religion and Science 2003–2022* (2020), accessed August 10, 2023, http://tinyurl.com/4prs2xsz; Stavros Lazaris, ed., *A Companion to Byzantine Science*, Brill Companions to the Byzantine World 6 (Leiden and Boston, MA: Brill, 2020); David C. Lindberg, "The Fate of Science in Patristic and

Medieval Christendom," in *The Cambridge Companion to Science and Religion*, ed. Peter Harrison (Cambridge: Cambridge University Press, 2010), 21–38; David C. Lindberg, *The Beginnings of Western Science: The European Scientific Tradition in Philosophical, Religious, and Institutional Context, Prehistory to A.D. 1450*, 2nd ed. (Chicago, IL and London: The University of Chicago Press, 2007), 148–50; Efthymios Nicolaidis, *Science and Eastern Orthodoxy: From the Greek Fathers to the Age of Globalization*, trans. Susan Emanuel (Baltimore, MD: The Johns Hopkins University Press, 2011), 1–39; D. S. Wallace-Hadrill, *The Greek Patristic View of Nature* (Manchester and New York: Manchester University Press and Barns & Noble, 1968).
9 See *Homilies on the Hexaemeron* 1.2.5–20.
10 For a summary of Ptolemaic cosmography, see David H. Kelley and Eugene F. Milone, *Exploring Ancient Skies: A Survey of Ancient and Cultural Astronomy*, 2nd ed., Astrophysics and Space Science Library 374 (New York: Springer, 2011), 244–48.
11 See *Homilies on the Hexaemeron* 1.3–4; 3.3. For notes on his approach, see Nicolaidis, *Science and Orthodoxy*, 9–10.
12 *Homilies on the Hexaemeron* 1.2.5–12.
13 Credit: Wikimedia Commons, accessed March 20, 2024, https://tinyurl.com/59xtw4sp.
14 Credit: The University of Sydney Library's Rare Books and Special Collections. Call number: Deane RB 4692.119, accessed March 20, 2024, https://tinyurl.com/2p839j7.
15 *An Apology for the Hexaemeron* 24.37.11–38.10; 28.41.12–42.6.
16 The relevant chapters are *An Apology for the Hexaemeron* 33.46.12–38.51.7.
17 See *An Apology for the Hexaemeron* 8–9, 64–74.
18 For example, see *Stromateis* 1.3.2; 1.32.1; 5.7.5–6; 6.80.1–3; 6.84.1–4.
19 See *An Exact Exposition on the Orthodox Faith*, 15–44.
20 The literature on their contributions is constantly growing. See, for example, Costache, *Humankind and the Cosmos*, 232, 322, 339, 367; Doru Costache, "Maximus the Confessor and John Damascene's Cosmology," in *The T&T Clark Handbook of Christian Theology and the Modern Sciences*, ed. John Slattery (Bloomsbury/T&T Clark, 2020), 81–91, esp. 90; Anne Tihon, "Alexandrian Astronomy in the 2nd Century ad: Ptolemy and His Times," in *The Alexandrian Tradition: Interactions between Science, Religion, and Literature*, ed. Luis Arturo Guichard, Juan Luis García Alonso, and María Paz de Hoz, Ricerche di cultura europea 28 (Bern and Berlin: Peter Lang, 2014), 73–91, esp. 74–77. For other examples of engaging the sciences positively, see Andrew Louth, "Basil and the Greek Fathers on Creation in the *Hexaemeron*," in *The T&T Clark Handbook of Christian Theology and the Modern Sciences*, 67–79; Andrew Louth, "The Six Days of Creation According to the Greek Fathers," in *Reading Genesis after Darwin*, ed. Stephen C. Barton and David Wilkinson (New York: Oxford University Press, 2009), 39–55. It has been observed, however, that exegetically conservative theologians, such as those of the Antiochian tradition, rejected the Ptolemaic system.

See Benjamin Gleede, "The Christian Rejection of Ptolemean Cosmography in (Late) Antiquity: Motives, Modalities, and Backgrounds," in *Platonism and Christianity in Late Ancient Cosmology: God, Soul, Matter*, ed. Ana Schiavoni-Palanciuc and Johannes Zachhuber, Ancient Philosophy & Religion 9 (Leiden and Boston, MA: Brill, 2022), 184–204, esp. 185–95.

21 See Doru Costache's studies, "Patristic and Neopatristic Antecedents of Scientifically Engaged Theology," *St Vladimir's Theological Quarterly* 67, no. 1–2 (2023): 115–45, esp. 133–145; "Theological Anthropology Today: Panayiotis Nellas's Contribution," in *Orthodox Christianity and Modern Science: Past, Present and Future*, ed. Kostas Tampakis and Haralampos Ventis, Science and Orthodox Christianity 3 (Turnhout: Brepols, 2022), 167–82; "A Theology of the World: Dumitru Stăniloae, the Traditional Worldview, and Contemporary Cosmology'," in *Orthodox Christianity and Modern Science: Tensions, Ambiguities, Potential*, ed. Vasilios N. Makrides and Gayle Woloschak, Science and Orthodox Christianity 1 (Turnhout: Brepols, 2019), 205–22.

22 See Costache, "Patristic and Neopatristic Antecedents," 143–44.

23 See Costache, *Humankind and the Cosmos*, 61–62.

24 See Costache, "Patristic and Neopatristic Antecedents," 134–44; "Theological Anthropology Today," 170–81; "A Theology of the World," 208–21.

25 Panayiotis Nellas, *Deification in Christ: Orthodox Perspectives on the Nature of the Human Person*, trans. Norman Russell, Contemporary Greek Theologians 5 (Crestwood, NY: St Vladimir's Seminary Press, 1997; original Greek edition, 1979).

26 See Nellas, *Deification in Christ*, 41–42.

27 See Nellas, *Deification in Christ*, 27, 28, 41–42, 98.

28 For a relevant discussion, see Costache, "Theological Anthropology Today," 168–70; Doru Costache, "The Orthodox Doctrine of Creation in the Age of Science," *Journal of Orthodox Christian Studies* 2, no. 1 (2019): 43–64, esp. 43–44.

29 The most familiar controversy focuses upon Richard Dawkins' book, *The God Delusion* (London: Bantam Press, 2006). From the many responses to this book, see Alister E. McGrath and Joanna Collicutt McGrath, *The Dawkins Delusion: Atheist Fundamentalism and the Denial of the Divine* (Downers Grove, IL: IVP Books, 2007), and David Bentley Hart, *Atheist Delusions: The Christian Revolution and Its Fashionable Enemies* (New Haven, CT and London: Yale University Press, 2009). Both sides spray vitriol on each other's face. For a relevant discussion, see Costache, "Patristic and Neopatristic Antecedents," 122–23.

30 Michael Hanby, "Questioning the Science and Religion Question," in *After Science and Religion: Fresh Perspectives from Philosophy and Theology*, ed. Peter Harrison, John Milbank, and Paul Tyson (Cambridge: Cambridge University Press, 2022), 155–70, esp. 167–69; Perry and Leidenhag, *Science-Engaged Theology*, 7–21; Paul Tyson, "Introduction: After Science and Religion?" in *After Science and Religion*, 1–11, esp. 2–6.

31 See Brent Smith, *Religious Studies and the Goal of Interdisciplinarity*, Routledge Focus (London and New York: Routledge, 2020), 1–18.
32 See Loretta Koertge, "Philosophy of the Social Sciences," in *The Philosophy of Science: An Encyclopedia*, ed. Sahotra Sarkar and Jessica Pfeifer (New York and London: Routledge, 2006), 780–85, esp. 782; Hans Radder, "Experiment," in *The Philosophy of Science*, 268–75, esp. 274.
33 Davison, "Science and Specificity," 236–37.
34 Perry and Leidenhag, *Science-Engaged Theology*, 48–62; Perry and Leidenhag, "What Is Science-Engaged Theology?," 248. John Wesley himself saw nature and the natural sciences worth considering theologically. See Daniel Pratt Morris-Chapman, "Beyond the Quadrilateral: The Place of Nature in John Wesley's Epistemology of Theology," *HTS Teologiese Studies/Theological Studies* 78, no. 2 (2022): 1–8, https://doi.org/10.4102/hts.v78i2.7643; Glen O'Brien, "'Creatures Capable of God': John Wesley's Theological Anthropology and the Posthuman Future," in *A Curious Machine: Wesleyan Reflections on the Posthuman Future*, ed. Arseny Ermakov and Glen O'Brien (Eugene, OR: Wipf and Stock, 2023), 13–32, esp. 14–15.
35 Carmody Grey, "A Theologian's Perspective on Science-Engaged Theology," *Modern Theology* 37, no. 2 (2021): 489–94, esp. 493–94. See also Peter Harrison, *The Territories of Science and Religion* (Chicago, IL and London: The University of Chicago Press, 2015), 21–54.
36 Cardinal John Henry Newman, *On the Scope and Nature of University Education*, Everyman's Library 723 (London and New York: Dent and Dutton, 1965), 55–79.
37 See Hanby, "Questioning the Science and Religion Question," 163–64. The most common case is the concept of laws of nature, whose origin is religious. See Paul Davies, *The Mind of God: Science and the Search for Ultimate Meaning* (London: Penguin Books, 1993), 73–78.
38 Lisa H. Sideris, "Religion," in *Handbook of the Anthropocene: Humans between Heritage and Future*, ed. Nathanaël Wallenhorst and Christoph Wulf (Cham: Springer, 2024), 905–10, esp. 905, https://doi.org/10.1007/978-3-031-25910-4_148.
39 Sideris, "Religion," 906. According to her, typical for such a quasi-religious idea of the Earth is Lovelock's "Gaia hypothesis" (907), whereas the correspondent view in terms of humanity's agency are the various formulations of the "noosphere" (907–08).
40 Newman, *Scope and Nature*, 30–54.
41 Perry and Leidenhag, "What Is Science-Engaged Theology?" 248.
42 See, for example, Paul's reference to the fundamental elements of the universe, after the ancient fashion, of course, in Colossians 2:8. See Tim Hegedus, *Early Christianity and Ancient Astrology*, Patristic Studies 6 (New York: Peter Lang, 2007), 224–26.
43 See Peter Harrison, "Science, Eastern Orthodoxy, and Protestantism," *Isis* 107, no. 3 (2016): 587–91; Vasilios N. Makrides, "The Natural Sciences in the Framework of a European History of Religion," in *Religion in Culture—Culture in Religion*, ed. Christoph Auffarth, Alexandra Grieser, and Anne Koch (Tübingen: Tübingen University Press, 2021), 271–94,

esp. 289–90; Efthymios Nicolaidis, Eudoxie Delli, Nikolaos Livanos, Kostas Tampakis, and George Vlahakis, "Science and Orthodox Christianity: An Overview," *Isis* 107, no. 3 (2011): 542–66; Nicolaidis, *Science and Eastern Orthodoxy*, 1–39, 55–105. See also the volumes that so far resulted from the project "Science and Orthodoxy around the World," run by the Institute of Historical Research of the National Hellenic Research Foundation, Athens (2017–2019): Kostas Tampakis and Haralampos Ventis, eds., *Orthodox Christianity and Modern Science: Past, Present and Future*, Science and Orthodox Christianity 3 (Turnhout: Brepols, 2022); Christopher C. Knight and Alexei V. Nesteruk, eds., *Orthodox Christianity and Modern Science: Theological, Philosophical, Scientific and Historical Aspects of the Dialogue*, Science and Orthodox Christianity 2 (Turnhout: Brepols, 2021); Vasilios N. Makrides and Gayle Woloschak, eds., *Orthodox Christianity and Modern Science: Tensions, Ambiguities, Potential*, Science and Orthodox Christianity 1 (Turnhout: Brepols, 2019).

44 Here are works that address, either fully or in part, Orthodox cosmology: Costache, "The Orthodox Doctrine of Creation," 50–58; Doru Costache, "Mapping Reality within the Experience of Holiness," in *The Oxford Handbook of Maximus the Confessor*, ed. Pauline Allen and Bronwen Neil (Oxford: Oxford University Press, 2015), 378–39; Foltz, *The Noetics of Nature*; Alexei V. Nesteruk, *The Sense of the Universe: Philosophical Explication of Theological Commitment in Modern Cosmology* (Minneapolis, MN: Fortress Press, 2015); Alexei V. Nesteruk, *Light from the East: Theology, Science, and the Orthodox Christian Tradition*, Theology and the Sciences (Minneapolis, MN: Fortress Press, 2003); Stoyan Tanev, *Energy in Orthodox Theology and Physics: From Controversy to Encounter* (Eugene, OR: Pickwick, 2017). See also the sources they reference.

45 Dumitru Stăniloae, *Theology and the Church*, trans. Robert Barringer (Crestwood, NY: St Vladimir's Seminary Press, 1980), 224.

46 Dumitru Stăniloae, "Introducere," in *Sfântul Atanasie cel Mare: Scrieri*, first part, ed. Dumitru Stăniloae, Părinți și Scriitori Bisericești 15 (București: Editura Institutului Biblic și de Misiune al Bisericii Ortodoxe Române, 1987), 5–26, esp. 24.

47 Apart from the only existing study of Stăniloae's views of science, quoted in n. 20, only sporadic references to his relevant contributions are available. See Daniel Ciobotea, "O dogmatică pentru omul de azi" (dogmatic theology for contemporary people), in *Dumitru Stăniloae sau Paradoxul Teologiei* (Dumitru Staniloae or the paradox of theology), ed. Theodor Baconsky and Bogdan Tătaru-Cazaban (București: Anastasia, 2003), 87–107, esp. 101–03; Adrian Lemeni, "References of Father Dumitru Stăniloae's Thought in the Dialogue between Theology and Science," in *Orthodox Christianity and Modern Science: Theological, Philosophical, Scientific and Historical Aspects of the Dialogue* (2021), 155–63; Nesteruk, *Light from the East*, 6, 9.

48 For a survey of relevant references in Stăniloae's original writings in Romanian, see Costache, "A Theology of the World."

49 Dumitru Stăniloae, *Teologia dogmatică ortodoxă*, three vols, 3rd ed. (București: Editura Institutului Biblic și de Misiune al Bisericii Ortodoxe Române, 2003), 1: 6. For an analysis of this passage within the context of Stăniloae's attitude to the sciences, see Costache, "Patristic and Neopatristic Antecedents," 134–38; Costache, "Strange Bedfellows," 10–11.

50 See Matyáš Havrda, *The So-Called Eighth Stromateus by Clement of Alexandria: Early Christian Reception of Greek Scientific Methodology*, Philosophia Antiqua 144 (Leiden and Boston, MA: Brill, 2017), 25–76; Matyáš Havrda, "Demonstrative Method in *Stromateis* VII: Context, Principles, and Purpose," in *The Seventh Book of the Stromateis: Proceedings of the Colloquium on Clement of Alexandria*, ed. Matyáš Havrda, Vít Hušek, and Jana Plátová, Supplements to Vigiliae Christianae 117 (Leiden and Boston, MA: Brill, 2012), 261–76.

51 See his *The Sense of the Universe* and *Light from the East*. See also Alexei V. Nesteruk, *The Universe as Communion: Towards a Neo-Patristic Synthesis of Theology and Science* (London: T&T Clark, 2008).

52 See Alexei V. Nesteruk, *The Universe in the Image of Imago Dei: The Dialogue between Theology and Science as a Hermeneutics of the Human Condition* (Eugene, OR: Pickwick, 2022) and "Humanity as the Central Theme of the Dialogue between Theology and Science," in *Orthodox Christianity and Modern Science: Past, Present and Future*, 147–66.

53 For a different solution to this issue, see Costache, *Humankind and the Cosmos*, chapter seven.

54 See relevant discussions from two prudent optimists belonging to different generations: Albert Einstein, "On the Method of Theoretical Physics," *Philosophy of Science* 1, no. 2 (1934): 163–69, esp. 168–69, https://doi.org/10.1086/286316; Stephen Hawking, *A Brief History of Time*, updated and expanded 10th anniversary ed. (New York: Bantam Books, 1996), 171–86.

55 While we shall address this topic several times in what follows, it is worth pointing out the very recent discussion of related matters in Tyson, "Learned Ignorance?" 4–6. See also Yuto Minami and Eiichiro Komatsu, "A Hint of New Physics in Polarized Radiation from the Early Universe," Max Planck Institute for Astrophysics (November 2020), accessed March 20, 2024, https://tinyurl.com/ycyat6tj.

56 For this attitude, see Jennifer E. Stellar, "Awe Helps Us Remember Why It Is Important to Forget the Self," *Annals of the New York Academy of Sciences* 1501, no. 1 (special issue): *The Power of Wonder: Modern Marvels in the Age of Science* (2021): 81–84, https://doi.org/10.1111/nyas.14577.

57 Tolkien, *The Lord of the Rings*, 129–30.

2 What We Know and What We Don't Know about the Universe

Scientific Perspectives

This subject raises primal questions, questions of origin and future and our place in this cold, dark cosmos. Here, we explore just what we know and what we don't know about the universe and the impact of current knowledge on our philosophical views of reality. Are the views of science and theology in conflict? Or is there an underlying harmony to seemingly disparate worldviews? Is there a way for theology, especially Orthodox theology, to integrate elements from contemporary cosmology into its view of things? While these questions constitute the backdrop of this undertaking, in what follows, we focus on matters specific to scientific cosmology.

Historical Preliminaries

In little more than a century,[1] our view of the universe has changed immeasurably. By the early 1900s, powerful telescopes had revealed that our Sun is just one of more than one hundred billion stars within our Milky Way galaxy. We now know that the Milky Way is just one of almost a trillion galaxies, each home to hundreds of billions of stars, within the observable universe. The immense scale of the cosmos means that light, travelling at a blistering 300,000 kilometres per second, takes four years to reach us from the nearest star, millions of years from the nearest galaxies, and more than ten billion years from the most distant objects we can observe. As far as we know, beyond the observable universe, the cosmos continues to infinity, with infinite numbers of galaxies and stars that will elude us forever (see Figure 2.1).

New technologies have opened the sky to rays invisible to our eyes. Radio telescopes have spied huge clouds of cold hydrogen gas throughout the galaxies and immense jets blasting over millions of light years. These jets reveal that the hearts of galaxies are home to immense black holes, completely collapsed objects whose intense gravitational fields can accelerate matter up to almost the speed of light. At the other end of the spectrum, X-ray and gamma-ray telescopes have spotted superhot and superdense stars that are extremely unlike our Sun and can only be the remnants of once-living stars. This reveals that the universe is a dynamic place, continually evolving and

DOI: 10.4324/9781003527138-2

Figure 2.1 The Hubble Ultra Deep Field. Released in 2004, this image from the Hubble Space Telescope represented more than eleven days of exposure to an apparently blank piece of sky. As well as a few stars in our cosmic backyard, this image contains almost ten thousand individual galaxies, a tiny fraction of the trillion galaxies out there in the observable universe.[2]

changing, with gas clouds collapsing to form new generations of stars that live out their lives over billions of years. Through stellar death, either as sedate expiration or violent explosion, matter gets recycled back into gas and then into the next generation of stars. We ourselves are built from the ashes of previous generations of stars.

Our telescopes have presented us with a spectacular view of the universe, from clusters of stars and colourful clouds of gas to a sea of galaxies stretching to the edge of the cosmos. Iconic images from the James Webb and Hubble Space Telescopes adorn walls and screensavers across the globe. But, the goal of science is to do more than look; the goal of science is to understand. Over the same century that our observations revealed the depth and beauty of the universe, advances in scientific theory sought to explain what we have seen. The resulting field of astrophysics is immense, incorporating the nuclear reactions at the hearts of stars, the chemistry of interstellar dust grains, the lives of galaxies, and the potential of life on other worlds, to name but a few.

Modern cosmology was born in the first few decades of the twentieth century. In 1915, Albert Einstein published his General Theory of Relativity,[3] a fiendishly complex mathematical idea that overturned the picture of gravity laid down by Isaac Newton more than two centuries before. Einstein realised that a rewrite of gravity was essential as Newton's approach was starting to fray, unable to describe the orbit of the planet Mercury accurately. He was spurred on as Newton's mathematics completely failed to mesh with his special theory, in which distance and time were shown to be malleable. Einstein was able to write gravity into the bending and stretching of space and time, accurately accounting for the motion of Mercury. Einstein's General Theory has proven to be very successful, even forming the basis for the Global Positioning System (GPS), which ensures we arrive at the correct destination and on time.

As gravity dominates on cosmic scales, Einstein explored whether his equations could account for the structure of the entire universe. But Einstein was a man of his time and had some particular views of the cosmos, assuming it was static and unchanging. Nevertheless, his equations suggested that the universe should be dynamic and changing. Disappointed, Einstein realised that his equations offered him a solution, a mathematical term that effectively added an antigravity that would act to stabilise the universe. Russian Alexander Friedmann felt this was unnecessary and that the obvious conclusion should be that we are living in an evolving universe. Einstein called Friedmann's mathematics "suspicious," but soon new observations would sway the issue.

In 1919, American Edwin Hubble arrived at the Mount Wilson Observatory in California to use the world's newest and largest telescope, the 100" Hooker. His goal was to survey the distant universe, measuring the positions and speeds of galaxies beyond our own Milky Way. This was an important step, as the existence of other galaxies as distinct entities was a matter of intense discussion. In 1920, the Great Debate[4] between Harlow Shapley and Heber Curtis was held, arguing whether the fuzzy nebulae spied through telescopes were just clouds of material within the Milky Way or were themselves "island universes."

To chart distances, Hubble used the power of the 100" telescope to search for Cepheid variable stars among the nebulae. These pulsing stars were the focus of Henrietta Swan Leavitt, working at the Harvard College Observatory around 1910. She found that the period of stellar blinking was implicitly correlated with true brightness, and once you know the true brightness of a star, you can calculate the distance from its apparent brightness. By 1929, Hubble had charted the distance to twenty-four nebulae, conclusively demonstrating that they were far beyond the edge of the galaxy. This greatly increased the measured scale of the universe and showed that the Milky Way was but one galaxy among many.

As well as measuring galactic distances, Hubble also measured galactic speeds, inferred from the stretching of their light to longer wavelengths, something known as the redshift. This use of the Doppler shift to measure the speeds of the nebulae had been demonstrated by Vesto Slipher only a few years previously, but with the distances in-hand Hubble was primed to revolutionise our understanding of the universe. In charting the galactic distances against their speeds, he discovered something quite unexpected: the further the distance to a particular galaxy, the faster it was moving. In fact, the two were roughly proportional to one another, so you could draw a straight line through them with a constant slope. This slope, which we now call the "Hubble Constant," has a measured value of around 70 km/s/Mpc, meaning that for every megaparsec (about three million light years of distance) that a galaxy is from us, it is moving 70 km/s faster! While Hubble did not realise it, he had discovered the precise signature of motion predicted in Friedmann's mathematics of the universe. In short, Hubble discovered that the universe is expanding.[5]

With the observations of Hubble and the theoretical work of Einstein and Friedmann, modern cosmology was born. In the century that has followed, we have learnt much more and have built an accurate picture of the life of the cosmos. Modern cosmology is a story of scientific success, an international endeavour that continues to explore the secrets of the universe. But cosmology is not complete, and cosmology is not perfect. The remainder of this chapter explores what we know and, importantly, what we don't know about the universe.

What Do We Know?

The Universe Had a Beginning

The link between Hubble's observations and the notion of an expanding universe was made by Belgian Catholic priest Georges Lemaitre.[6] He realised that expansion results in the distances between any two galaxies in the universe increasing in time, so that tomorrow the galaxies will be further apart than today; this separation of galaxies will, therefore, continue to increase into the future. Lemaitre also realised that two galaxies would have been closer together yesterday and would have been closer and closer the more we looked back into the past. Eventually, if we look back far enough, we will find that the distance between the galaxies would have been zero. We have arrived at a cosmic starting point. Lemaitre called this universal birth the "Cosmic Egg"; today, we call it the "Big Bang."[7]

By reversing the expansion, Lemaitre calculated that the universe began about two billion years ago, an enormous timescale compared to the millennia of human civilisation. Lemaitre did not know it, but Hubble had underestimated the distances to galaxies, misled by precisely what variable stars he was observing. Once corrected, the age of the universe was estimated to be more than ten billion years, and currently, with accurate measurements of the expansion and content of the cosmos, we know it was born almost fourteen billion years ago.

The conditions of the early universe were very different from the cosmos today, with immense densities and temperatures as things were initially squeezed tightly together. Initially, there was no normal matter, with everything ripped into its subatomic components. The universe was a sea of high-energy radiation, electrons, and quarks. While these conditions were extreme compared to everyday experiences, we can understand the properties of the very early universe through our equations of nuclear and particle physics. As the universe expanded and cooled, the collisions between particles became less violent, and the quarks could bind together into protons and neutrons, the building blocks of normal atoms. Once the universe was a few minutes old, it was cool enough for protons and neutrons to join into the first chemical elements, but the cooling was rapid, and this nucleosynthesis of elements rapidly came to an end. This primordial mix of elements in the moments after the cosmic birth was around seventy-five per cent hydrogen, twenty-five per cent helium, and a smattering of other light elements.

As well as the matter that made up the first elements, the early universe was bathed in a sea of ultra-hot radiation, gamma-rays and X-rays, with enough energy to tear matter apart. As the universe expanded, this radiation also cooled to less energetic wavelengths through optical light and to longer wavelength radio waves. This radiation is still with us today, cooled to 2.75 K above absolute zero. The existence of this background radiation was predicted by the theoretical work of Ralph Alpher and George Gamow in 1948, as they calculated the physics of the infant universe, but their work was not known by Arno Penzias and Robert Wilson when they stumbled across it during their observations in 1965. Today, detailed observations from several space-based telescopes have accurately mapped this leftover radiation, which is important evidence that our universe was born in a hot Big Bang.

The Universe Has Evolved and Changed

After the nuclear furnaces of the first few minutes, the universe continued to expand and cool. The background radiation faded away, and the universe entered what is known as the Dark Ages. Matter was still hot, with electrons unbound from atomic nuclei, but by almost four hundred thousand years after the beginning, matter was cool enough for normal atoms to finally form. In the darkness, gravity was drawing matter together, pooling into the formation sites of galaxies. As gas collapsed, its density increased, with clouds eventually fragmenting into smaller chunks. The gravitational collapse of these smaller chunks continued, with the density and temperatures of their central cores soaring. Eventually, at temperatures of many millions of degrees, nuclear reactions sparked, with hydrogen being fused into helium, liberating huge quantities of energy. At around two hundred million years old, the first stars were born, and the universe was again bathed in light.[8]

The first stars were unlike the stars in the universe today. Being pure hydrogen and helium, these stars were probably huge, a hundred times more massive than the Sun, with their nuclear furnaces burning furiously. Similar stars we know of eat through their nuclear fuel quickly, fusing it into heavier and heavier elements, and end their lives as supernovae, exploding stars that rip themselves to pieces. Their matter is spewed back into interstellar space, polluting it with the heavier elements created in their nuclear cores. This stellar ash is then recycled into the next generation of stars. The presence of heavier elements influences the formation of stars, with smaller, more stable stars being born. Importantly for us, these heavier elements can condense into planets orbiting the stars, the site essential for the formation of life in the universe.

All the while, gravity was at work, drawing more and more matter together. The first fragments of mass, protogalaxies, continued to grow as matter rained down. Eventually, protogalactic chunks collided and amalgamated, building larger and larger galaxies. This "hierarchical" growth continued as larger galaxies consumed smaller galaxies, tearing them apart and adding their stars to their own. Around ten billion years ago, our Milky Way was born, becoming a rapidly growing galaxy among the others. Since then, it has continued to grow, cannibalising smaller systems that came too close. This process continues, with smaller galaxies steadily being consumed and being disrupted by the intense gravitational pull of the Milky Way. About five billion years ago, in a collapsing gas cloud, our Sun was born, generations after the first stars had burst into life. Within the swirling disk of gas that accompanied its formation, the Earth condensed.

In other places in the universe, the collapse of mass was more dramatic. The process is still unclear, but we assume that, there, inordinate quantities of matter—several hundred million times the mass of the Sun—were poured into a very small volume. With so much matter, the intense gravitational field inexorably continued to collapse until it was complete, with all matter driven to a single point, forming a black hole. These immense black holes still dot the universe, sitting at the hearts of galaxies and continuing to draw in more matter. As this captured material swirls around before its final dive into the black hole, it grows intensely hot and can outshine the hundreds of billions of stars in the rest of the galaxy. These hyperactive galaxies, known as quasars, were much more common in the early universe but are rarer today. These monsters are still out there in the universe and will continue to glow as matter is fed to them.

The Universe Is Dominated by the Dark Side

Telescopes see light, be it in the same visible range that our eyes are sensitive to or radio waves and X-rays that we cannot see directly. By carefully adding up all of the sources of light, astronomers can weigh the universe, calculating just how much mass is out there. While in the early decades of the last century there were hints of something strange, by the late 1960s it was clear that there was a problem; most of the universe's mass was missing. The name most associated with this discovery is of American Vera Rubin,[9] whose key insights came from the motions of stars in galaxies. In the Solar System, the Earth is held in its orbit by the gravitational pull of the Sun. More than that, the speed of the Earth in its orbit is set precisely by how hard the Sun tugs on it. Rubin and colleagues were looking at how stars orbited within various galaxies, especially our nearest large neighbour, the Andromeda galaxy. Stars were clearly zipping around at more than two hundred kilometres per second, but when Rubin calculated just how much mass was present by adding up the starlight, there was nowhere near enough to account for this speed. Moreover, the speeds of stars in their orbits did not slow as she considered orbits further and further away from the galactic centre, a situation very unlike the Solar System where planets travel more slowly the further away from the Sun they are. Rubin concluded that there must be more mass there, invisible to our telescopes, emitting no light whatsoever. And not only that but there must be at least six times more of this dark matter than luminous mass.[10]

Since the 1970s, dark matter has appeared everywhere we have looked. It dominates not only the motions of stars within galaxies but the motions of galaxies themselves, with astronomers detecting the extra gravitational influence of dark matter as galaxies flow and collide. Astronomers have used other tools to search for the presence of dark matter, including its impact on the overall cosmic expansion, finding that the luminous matter is simply insufficient to account for the expansion we see. Another approach comes from Einstein's general relativity, which predicts that the path of light through the universe will be impacted by the presence of masses, resulting in a distorted, multiply-imaged view of the distant cosmos. Again, when calculating the amount of mass required to produce the distorted view of the cosmos we see, astronomers concluded that there is an immense quantity of dark matter out there, and all the stars, gas, planets, and people are just minor players in the universe.

The discovery of dark matter was surprising, but at the end of the 1990s, the discovery of dark energy was completely startling. The key observations came from exploding stars—supernovae—in the distant universe. Astronomers were on a quest to chart the expansion rate and history of the universe, as this would reveal what the universe contains. This might sound a little strange, but the presence of mass in the universe acts like a decelerator on cosmic expansion, slowing it down over billions of years. However, deceleration was not what astronomers saw. They found that the expansion of the universe was speeding up! Such acceleration was quite unexpected as matter, both luminous and dark, produces deceleration, as does the presence of light and radiation. To account for the observed expansion, astronomers concluded there must be another energy source in the universe, promptly called "dark energy," whose properties were unlike normal matter. This stuff must possess a tension, the opposite of pressure, which has the right characteristics to drive expansion faster.

The most surprising thing about dark energy is just how much there must be, with it dominating the cosmic energy budget. In total, seventy per cent of the universe must be dark energy, with twenty-five per cent dark matter, while all the stars and gas and planets and people are a paltry five per cent. In a little more than fifty years, the universe of atoms, the stuff from which we are made, has become nothing but a cosmic sideshow, and the universe is truly dominated by what goes on in the dark. Dark energy, however, has one final insult. Unlike matter, which is continually thinned as the universe expands, as a result of its peculiar properties, the density of dark energy remains constant. This means that, in the future, the presence of matter will become steadily less important as the influence of dark energy comes to dominate the cosmic stage completely.

The Universe Is Winding Down

In 1852, William Thomson Kelvin coined the phrase "the heat death of the universe." Lord Kelvin was a central player in the field of thermodynamics, which studies the flow of heat from one place to another. Driven by the Industrial Revolution and the invention of steam engines, people wondered about efficiency and how much energy from burning coal and wood could be turned into useful work. The conclusion was stark: perfect efficiency was unobtainable, and some energy had to be lost as sound and warmth to the environment. This growth of degraded energy is related to the concept of entropy, often described as the amount of disorder in a system. To Kelvin, the system was the entire universe.

Kelvin was working at a time long before the notion of a universal birth, or before we understood that the Sun is powered by nuclear reactions, but he realised the fact that, based on the growth of entropy, the entire universe must be winding down. Let's consider sunlight, which has a high density of useful energy. Sunlight can make its way through the food chain, being absorbed by plants, eaten by herbivores, and eventually by carnivores, including ourselves. While the total amount of energy might remain the same, at every step of the process, energy is downgraded. As you read these words, your body is emitting infrared radiation, a downgraded version of the sunlight absorbed by the plants.

And it is not just our Sun. All the stars are turning concentrated nuclear energy into starlight, building up heavier elements in the process. Some stars die spectacularly, blasting their material back into space, but most simply fizzle out, locking up their matter and preventing its recycling into new stars. There will come a time, many billions of years from now, when there will be no more raw material for stars, and no more will be born. Eventually, the remaining stars will begin to die, with the smallest ones holding out for more than a hundred trillion years. There will come a day when the last star will die, however, and the universe will again descend into the night. And, one might assume, the night will go on forever.

However, this is not the end of the universe. On immense timescales, $\sim 10^{30}$ years, physicists think that even matter will lose stability, and the atoms that make up all of us, now locked in long-dead stellar hearts, will finally melt into the darkness. On even longer timescales, $\sim 10^{100}$ years, Stephen Hawking postulated that even black holes will eventually evaporate. After this, the universe will be a tenuous sea of ever-cooling, ever-diluting radiation and electrons. No useful energy will be available for anything as complex as life, and the heat death of the universe will have arrived.[11]

What Don't We Know?

So far, we have looked at the successes of modern cosmology, but it would be wrong to think that there is an end to research and that there is nothing left to learn. We definitely know more than we did a few short decades ago, but there are worrying holes in our understanding. For example, we do not know why the universe is the way it is.[12] There is no definitive list of our current unknowns, but some of the biggest questions are as follows.

We Don't Know Where the Universe Comes from

Was the Big Bang the true beginning of the universe? As discussed, Lemaitre was the first to rewind the expansion of the cosmos and identify a specific starting point, but does this mean that the universe somehow sprang from a true nothing, a nothing of no time and no space? This "universe from nothing" remains a point of argument among both physicists and philosophers, being highly unsatisfactory in terms of explaining the universe's existence.[13]

There is currently a problem with fundamental physics that prevents us from pinpointing the true birth of the universe. As we look back in time, when the universe was hotter and denser, we rely on finer and finer physics to explain what was happening, from atomic through nuclear to fundamental particles. Before about 10^{-6} seconds, we know that our theories are not perfect, but we can push back with what we know to around 10^{-40} seconds where we hit a brick wall. At this point, the universe is so hot and so dense that the two key theories of modern physics—gravity through Einstein's relativity and the other forces through quantum mechanics—are vying for dominance. And we simply have not found the mathematics that allows us to describe this situation. Not for want of trying, as this search for a Theory of Everything has occupied many of the great minds of physics for many years.

If we crack the mathematics of the Theory of Everything, what might we find? We could discover that the Big Bang was the ultimate beginning, and we will just have to live with that. Others have speculated that our universe might be just one in an infinite sequence of universes that are born, live, and die, only to be reborn again. Or possibly ours is a daughter universe, born with many others from violent events, such as the formation of black holes, within a parent universe. That parent, too, could also be a daughter, with universes spawned in some semi-evolutionary sequence over an infinite time.

Others have a grander proposal that our universe is just one of an almost infinite number of universes in some *über*-universe known as the multiverse. This idea comes from one of the contenders for the Theory of Everything, namely, M-theory (although it appears that no one remembers what the M stands for). The multiverse is multidimensional, having maybe eleven, maybe more dimensions, in which our four-dimensional universe floats like a sheet in the wind, surrounded by other universes. What generates universes within the multiverse remains a mystery, but in the same way that the Sun has been steadily displaced from the centre of the universe over the eons, we might find that our universe is just one of many in the overarching multiverse.

The Dark Side Remains a Mystery

Dark matter and dark energy dominate the universe. Dark matter provides the gravitational framework in which galaxies and stars can form, while dark energy is driving the universal expansion faster and faster. Our everyday matter, formed from atoms, is essentially going along for the ride. But despite its dominance, the actual nature of either of these dark components remains mysterious.[14]

Dark matter is thought to be a fundamental particle, a currently unknown member of the particle physics zoo that contains the electrons and quarks that form the matter we are familiar with. The mathematics of particle physics has proven extremely successful in explaining fundamental interactions, for example, the myriad of particles thrown out in experiments such as the Large Hadron Collider. But within this mathematics there is no obvious place for a candidate for a dark matter particle. This has led physicists to propose a range of different mathematical extensions to the standard model of particle physics, each with new possible candidates that could be dark matter. The current problem facing physicists is to devise experiments that can reveal which of these might be correct and, hence, uncover the true nature of dark matter. At the time of writing, all experiments have yielded nothing conclusive, and dark matter remains mysterious.

The nature of dark energy, likewise, is essentially unknown. The cosmological equations tell us its bulk properties but offer no clues about its fundamental source. Some physicists have suggested that maybe dark energy is a property of the quantum vacuum, a strange consequence of virtual particles popping in and out of existence, but, while attractive, theoretical expectations and observation limits differ by $\sim 10^{120}$, the largest discrepancy in all of physics. Others have suggested that dark energy is something else, a field of energy related to the birth of the universe that might change with time. Again, the race is on to establish the imprint of evolving dark energy on astronomical observations and highlight just what dark energy truly is. Until evidence is obtained, the nature of dark energy remains hidden.

The mysterious nature of the dark sector has led some physicists to propose that we need to return to the drawing board. The problem, they say, is not the existence of strange substances in the universe but a failure in our physical theories to describe the universe. The suggestion is that Einstein's general theory of relativity is only an approximation of a true gravitational theory, which we have yet to discover. Once we have this new theory in hand, it will be able to describe the motions of stars and the expansion of the universe with reliance on any dark side components. Presently, this remains a fringe topic within modern physics, with the majority focused on the search for physical dark matter and dark energy; modern physics works just too well to imagine that the basic rules need to be radically altered. But if experiments continue to yield null results, with no clues to their presence, we may be forced to take these ideas more seriously.

We Don't Understand Why the Universe Is the Way It Is

Our mathematical theories of the universe depend on quantities we must measure from nature. As an example, the speed of light, usually represented as c in equations, can be found in electromagnetism, relativity, and quantum mechanics, but the equations do not tell us what value c is. To determine this, we undertook experiments and found that light travels at almost three hundred thousand kilometres per second. This is true not only regarding the speed of light. Our theories fail to predict other key aspects of the universe, including the masses of fundamental particles, such as the electrons and quarks, and the strengths of fundamental forces.

Why do these numbers, known as fundamental constants, have the values they do?[15] We do not know, but physicists can play "what if" games and consider other alternative universes where these constants take on different values. The results are stark, showing that small changes to the fundamental constants could result in a universe that is dead and sterile, unable to host the

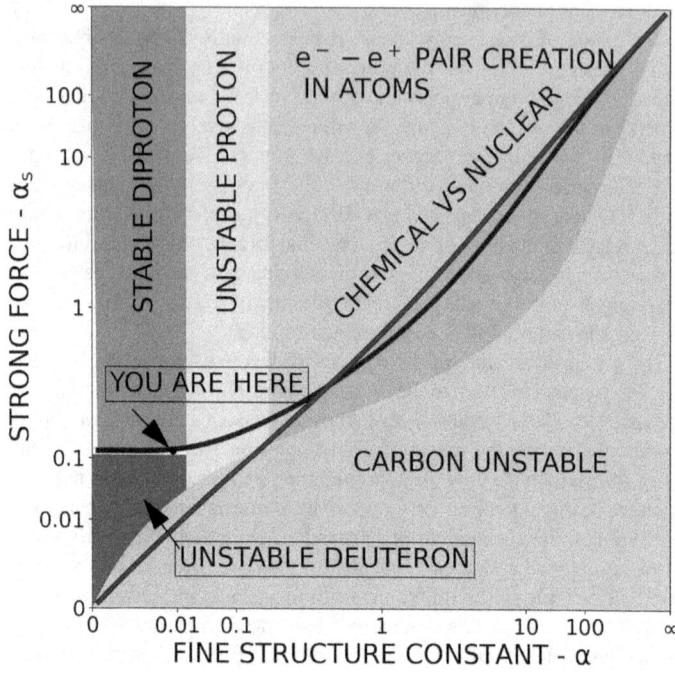

Figure 2.2 An Example of Cosmological Fine-Tuning. This considers the strength of the fine structure constant, responsible for the electromagnetic interaction, and the strong force that holds the nucleus of our atoms together. Our universe is marked as "You are here" in a sliver where the combinations of parameters allow the universe to be habitable. Other combinations result in the universe being robbed of the complexity that is essential for any form of life.[16]

complexity required for life. As an example, increasing the mass of a particular quark, the down quark, by a few percent robs the universe of neutrons. Without these, no element more complex than hydrogen is possible, and the universe would lack a periodic table, so no molecules, no planets, and no life (see Figure 2.2 for an example).

As physicists explore more deeply, they find that more properties of the universe—from its rate of expansion, the amount of dark energy, and even the tiny lumpiness of the matter soon after the Big Bang—are fine-tuned. For many of these, unimaginably small variations would render the universe completely uninhabitable. Out of all the imaginable universes, only a vanishingly small fraction would be able to host any kind of complex life. The question is why.

Of course, the simple solution is to state the obvious, that our universe is just the way it is, and to assert that talk of other universes is little more than fairy tales. Imaginative thinkers have turned to a theological solution, suggesting that our universe is fine-tuned due to the presence of a fine-tuner, while others have wondered if our universe is a computational simulation in some higher universe. The notion of the multiverse offers another potential solution, with the suggestion that each universe is written with its own distinct laws of physics and physical properties written into it when it is born. In this picture, most of the universes in the multiverse possess a mix of physics that makes them sterile. We find ourselves in one of the few universes that can support us, as we could not exist anywhere else, something known as anthropic selection. With so many dead universes, the wastefulness of the multiverse makes some uncomfortable, and the lack of any way to test their existence causes many physicists to question whether the multiverse is even science at all.

Do We Really Know Where the Universe Is Going?

The notion of the heat death suggests a very sombre end to our universe, steadily fading into nothingness where even time will eventually cease to have any real meaning. It means that life in the universe, our very existence, is but a brief moment in the Sun before the cosmos descends into a perpetual night.

Of course, our predictions for the future history of the universe are based upon the laws of physics as we currently understand them, and it is certain that these are incomplete. But, while there might be uncertainty in the specifics, the second law of thermodynamics and the growth of entropy are impossible to avoid. The universe is destined to run down. But is this the only possible future for the cosmos?[17]

We started this part of the chapter by pointing out that we don't understand where our universe comes from and that many feel that this solitary universe is not all there is or will ever be. Maybe the formation of black holes within our own universe has spawned uncountable other universes, and while ours eventually fades away, the daughter universes will continue. However, the saving grace for this universe might be the thing that appears to be driving it apart, namely, the existence of dark energy.

At the present time, dark energy has properties that result in accelerated cosmic expansion. But what if dark energy is not a constant and, in the future, changes its spot? What if it starts to induce contraction rather than expansion? Instead of things flying apart, they will be drawn together into the opposite of a Big Bang, a Big Crunch. The details of what would happen to the universe within such a cosmic crunch are obscure, but some have speculated that it could result in a bounce, a rebirth of the entire universe. Life in this universe would never survive such a crunch, but within a reborn cosmos, life might again have the chance to flourish.

There is another option for cosmic rebirth, but we would have to wait a long time for it to eventuate. Dark energy is present in a particular amount in every cubic metre within the universe. We don't know why it has the energy density it does, but it appears to be related to quantum mechanical aspects of space itself. Physicists have wondered if dark energy represents a "false vacuum," truly empty space that contains energy density as some barrier is preventing it from dissipating. If the universe were defined by the rules of classical physics, dark energy would be stuck in this state, unchanging for eternity. But quantum mechanics offers a way out. Known as quantum tunnelling, this allows energy to pour through the barrier, with dark energy moving closer to a true empty vacuum state. The energy released will possess the quality of being able to drive a new epoch of accelerated expansion, with the potential for multiple universes to be spawned in the event. However, the universe will have to wait a long time, an inconceivably long time, for the remotest chance of ever occurring, well into the heat death of the universe. Again, current life will be long gone, but there remains the possibility for universal rebirth.

Conclusions

This chapter opened with the recognition that modern cosmology, founded on observations with powerful telescopes coupled with leading theories of fundamental physics, represents a success of the scientific endeavour. All the evidence points to us inhabiting a universe that is almost fourteen billion years old and that was formed in a cataclysmic event we call the Big Bang. Since then, the universe has been constantly expanding and cooling, evolving and changing, causing the formation of galaxies, stars, planets, life, and eventually people. Cosmic evolution is not over and will continue into the future, as stars burn hydrogen into heavier elements. Eventually, this nuclear fuel will be exhausted, and the universe will plunge into darkness, fading away into eternity as it approaches a seemingly inevitable heat death.

As humans, we acknowledge our own mortality in the knowledge that, as a species and as a culture, we will live on. The mortality of the universe, with no endless future laid out for us, represents little more than cold comfort. However, our physical understanding of the universe is not complete regarding where our universe has come from and where it is going. We lack an understanding of what the dominant components of the universe actually are or why our universe possesses the particular combination of properties that allow us to be here. The search is on for the next level of physical theory—the Theory of Everything—that may pull back the curtain and reveal the answer to the most fundamental of questions. And written within it might be our universe's place in the overall scheme of universes, be it just one step within an ever-playing cycle from cosmic birth to cosmic death and back again.

Alternatively, we might establish that our universe is just one of countless other universes within an all-encompassing multiverse with its own rules governing cosmic life cycles.

Modern cosmology tells us that humans, on a small planet orbiting a normal star in a typical galaxy, will only be here for the briefest moment in the lifespan of the cosmos. We live in a time where there is abundant starlight and elements that allow us to exist. In the distant universe, it seems, when these conditions would have been changed, we will be gone. But long after our passing, and long into its future history, maybe, just maybe, our universe will be reborn. And one wonders, what do philosophers and theologians—including Orthodox theologians—think about the nature and the future of the universe and of ourselves? It is to this we turn in the next two chapters of this book.

Notes

1. It has been quite a century. For summaries, see Malcolm Longair's *The Cosmic Century* (Cambridge University Press, 2013) and Jim Peeble's *Cosmology's Century* (Princeton University Press 2020).
2. Credit: NASA, ESA, and S. Beckwith (STScI) and the HUDF Team, accessed 10 January 2024, https://esahubble.org/images/heic0406a/.
3. Einstein's life and scientific contributions are beautifully described in Abraham Pais' *Subtle Is the Lord: The Science and Life of Albert Einstein* (Oxford: Oxford University Press, 2005). See also Walter Isaacson's *Einstein: His Life and Universe* (New York: Simon & Schuster, 2007).
4. The great debate has been said to have been neither a debate nor even great, but it does mark an important step in us unveiling the scale of the universe. Details of the debate and its implications can be found at https://apod.nasa.gov/debate/debate20.html, accessed 15 March 2023.
5. As ever, history is often more complex than laid out in textbooks; who discovered the expanding universe and when is not Hubble's story alone. A recent summary can be found in Helge Kragh, "Hubble Law or Hubble-Lemaître Law? The IAU Resolution," https://arxiv.org/abs/1809.02557. The expansion of the universe has recently come under scrutiny. See Lucas Lombriser, "Cosmology in Minkowski Space," *Classical and Quantum Gravity* 40, no. 15 (2023), https://doi.org/10.1088/1361-6382/acdb41.
6. Nobel prize winner Steven Weinberg's, *The First Three Minutes: A Modern View of the Origin of the Universe*, updated ed. (New York: Basic Books, 1993) remains a classic description of the earliest moments of our universe. A recent update on this story can be found in Dan Hooper's *At the Edge of Time: Exploring the Mysteries of Our Universe's First Seconds* (Princeton, NJ: Princeton University Press, 2020).
7. For the saga of this phrase, see Helge Kragh, "How the Big Bang Got Its Name," *Nature* 627 (2024): 726–28, https://doi.org/10.1038/d41586-024-00894-z.

8 A recent description of the life of the first stars and galaxies can be found in Emma Chapman's *First Light* (Bloomsbury, 2021).
9 See Alan Lightman and Roberta Brower, *Origins: The Lives and Worlds of Modern Cosmologists* (Cambridge, MA: Harvard University Press, 1990), 285–305.
10 Brian Clegg's *Dark Matter & Dark Energy: The Hidden 95% of the Universe* (Icon, 2019) presents a recent review of the dark side.
11 The future history of the universe can look very bleak. Fred Adams and Greg Laughlin walk through the key features of a future cosmos in *The Five Ages of the Universe: Inside the Physics of Eternity* (New York: Simon & Schuster, 2000). A slightly older and more popular view is presented in Paul Davies' *The Last Three Minutes* (New York: Basic Books, 1997).
12 Geraint F. Lewis and Luke A. Barnes, *A Fortunate Universe: Life in a Finely Tuned Cosmos* (Cambridge: Cambridge University Press, 2016), 5.
13 The origin of the universe remains mysterious, and books on the topic often are written with an agenda in mind. Useful readings include Laurence Krauss' *A Universe from Nothing: Why Is There Something Rather Than Nothing* (Atria, 2013); Paul Steinhardt and Neil Turok's *Endless Universe: Beyond the Big Bang* (Doubleday, 2007); John Barrow's *New Theories of Everything: The Quest for Ultimate Explanation* (Oxford: Oxford University Press, 2007); Lee Smolin's *Life of the Cosmos* (Oxford: Oxford University Press, 1997), although there are numerous others. Note that not everyone is happy with this profusion of ideas, many of them are untestable and so are currently outside the domain of science. For an alternative view of modern physics and the obsession with a Theory of Everything, see Sabine Hossenfelder's *Lost in Math: How Beauty Leads Physics Astray* (New York: Basic Books, 2018); Peter Woit's *Not Even Wrong: The Failure of String Theory and the Continuing Challenge to Unify the Laws of Physics* (London: Vintage, 2011); Lee Smolin's *The Trouble with Physics: The Rise of String Theory, the Fall of Science, and What Comes Next* (London: Penguin, 2008).
14 For a review, see Dan Hooper's *Dark Cosmos: In Search of Our Universe's Missing Mass and Energy* (Harper Perennial, 2007).
15 This is a topic that generates much argument in physics circles. A detailed discussion of the question of fine-tuning and our place in the universe can be found in John Barrow and Frank Tipler's *The Anthropic Cosmological Principle* (Oxford: Oxford University Press, 1988), as well as in Lewis and Barnes, *A Fortunate Universe*.
16 Image modified from Lewis and Barnes, *A Fortunate Universe*, 75, with Lewis' permission; originally from Tegmark (1998).
17 Possible ends to our universe have recently been described by Katie Mack in her book *The End of Everything (Astrophysically Speaking)* (Allen Lane, 2020).

3 What We Know and What We Don't Know about the Universe
Theological Perspectives

The reader will notice in what follows a change of perspective and tone from the previous chapter. This has to do with the nature of theology's discourse, whose criteria differ significantly from the objectivist approach of scientific cosmology. And since this book proposes an exercise in science-engaged theology after the fashion of the Orthodox Christian tradition, this change is, we hope, fit for purpose. It seems to be, furthermore, the best way of tackling matters that pertain to the story of the self, with which we will be concerned primarily in Chapter Four, but also here, albeit in a limited manner.

The inner world—that is, thinkers' views, emotions, values, and aspirations—is integral to the humanities, including philosophy, semiotics, and theology, regardless of how rigours their methods tend to be.[1] The theological quest, therefore, unlike the current scientific method, is subjective as well as objective. Truth be told, the scientific method itself, while striving to remain objective as much as humanly possible, cannot entirely exclude subjectivity, the scientists' assumptions, errors, limitations, and goals;[2] hence, the need for peer review and feedback as necessary steps towards securing objectivity, including for the mathematics required by the natural sciences (see Figure 3.1). Even so, faith in the validity of the scientific method is a matter of personal conviction and choice; to an extent, it is as subjective as theologians' conviction that their discourse conveys divine wisdom. But theology does not claim utter objectivity, at least not if it remains aware of its own parameters.

Notoriously, for more than a millennium, the early Christian and medieval authors—initiators of an intellectual pursuit that led to the formation of the Orthodox worldview—consistently included in the prologues of their treatises caveats about people's limited capacity to capture the truth.[3] These caveats amount to saying that theologians must be aware that they process information, whether divinely revealed, traditionally received, or scientifically obtained, through the filter of their own personal values, education, experiences, and traditional commitments.[4] One understands in proportion to what one knows and is. With the traditional commitments mentioned above, another level of subjectivity becomes apparent. The earliest Christian authors were primarily interested in articulating the apostolic framework of their

DOI: 10.4324/9781003527138-3

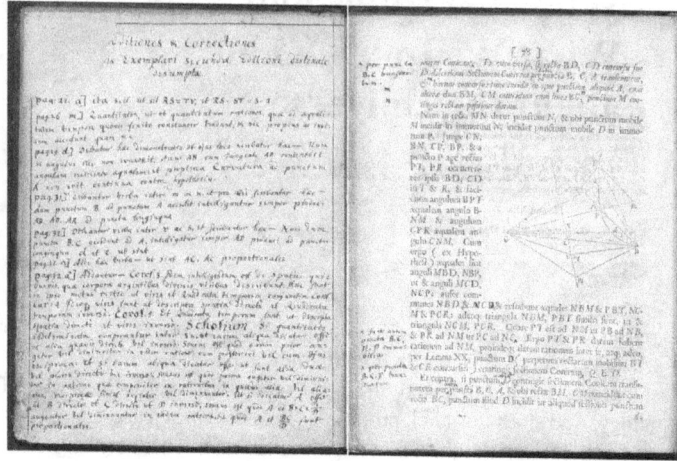

Figure 3.1 An Early Example of Scientific Peer Review. The images show pages from the first edition of Isaac Newton's *Philosophiae naturalis principia mathematica* ("Mathematical principles of natural philosophy"; London, 1686), which include notes and corrections in preparation for the second edition. Newton had sent copies of the book to colleagues across Europe for peer review and feedback. The images show notes in the hand of John Craig, a Scottish mathematician who helped Newton, and his assistant, Roger Cotes, to organise the feedback received and to prepare the revised edition of the book.[5]

thinking, the "rule of faith,"[6] and strived to maintain faithfulness to the criteria of Jesus' immediate disciples. This interest of mainstream or "apostolic" Christians resulted in the collection of writings known as Scripture or Bible, as well as in the production of related texts.[7] What matters is that choosing this framework was deliberate, out of several possibilities available, corresponding to the Scriptures that illustrate the criteria and the aspirations of these Christians, not the views of other groups. As such, there is nothing objective to this choice.

There is more to theology's subjectivity than this—yet another level, entirely personal but telling in regard to the method at work. Augustine of Hippo captures the situation with clarity, saying, "it is in you, my soul, that I measure the times."[8] In physical terms, the arrow of time still points towards the future, inexorably, but, according to Augustine, the fact of observing the flow of time enriches it. The objective knowledge of external realities is deepened and intensified by the observers who refer all things to their own perceptions and emotions. Inner worlds and outer worlds intersect and hold together. To the point, it is in their mind and through the lens of their faith experiences that theologians measure the knowns and the unknowns of the universe, reality's mystery.

As mystery, indeed, do Orthodox theologians perceive the vast cosmic vistas revealed by the modern sciences and the technological means at their disposal. They consider the universe through the *apophatic* lens they usually apply to divine mysteries. Christos Yannaras understands the apophatic approach as "refusal to exhaust knowledge of the truth in its formulation."[9] We take apophaticism as the humble disposition to renounce the anthropocentric rationalist claim that people can exhaust reality with intellectual devices and technological tools. We shall have more to say about this in Chapter Four. What matters is that the apophatic approach is not reductionist. In the words of Vladimir Lossky, "we shall need a sort of apophaticism in reverse in order to arrive at the revealed truth of creation," that is, an apophatic turn towards the cosmos, from its usual direction, godwards.[10] Lossky's reversed apophaticism was already known to early Christian thinkers such as Clement of Alexandria and John Chrysostom.[11] What modern Orthodox theologians timidly suggest as a "might be the case" was once a given.

In this light, irrespective of how much they know and don't know about the universe, Orthodox theologians are conditioned to contemplate it apophatically, as mystery. It should be noted that apophaticism, albeit a matter of personal preference, does not reduce reality to subjective impressions and ethereal perspectives. It is neither a matter of siding with the spiritualists against the materialists, to paraphrase Pierre Teilhard de Chardin's summary of Western thought,[12] nor a matter of cultivating irrational representations of the world. True, as we have seen in what came before, theology interprets reality from the viewpoint of subjective experiences, including spirituality, the latter understood as a personal, participatory, and relational grasp of reality. But the apophatic, or humble, approach amounts to a comprehensive grasp of things that does not exclude other perspectives; indeed, it welcomes them. The assumption that reality escapes any given method of observing or articulating it frees apophatic theology of methodological reductionism and predisposes it to cooperative, interdisciplinary undertakings.

As we have seen in the previous chapter, contemporary cosmologists appear to have adopted a similar cast of mind, although many still deny subjective experiences any significant role in the search for knowledge and understanding. In the words of Paul Tyson, they are still captive to the Kantian dogma of "limits of knowledge,"[13] which itself spells out subjective convictions. What matters is the acknowledgment that, regardless of how many things we have so far discovered about the universe, we still know extremely little. More than ninety percent of it eludes us, cosmologists calculate. This is a humble admission of limitations, an apophatic stance about reality as mystery.[14] The warning of Newman against science's capacity to deplete the mystery of the universe, be it by Newton's effort or someone else's,[15] holds therefore. In the same vein, and closer to home, Nesteruk points out that "the more that cosmology refines its scenario of the universe's evolution, the more it realises the abyss of the physically unknown."[16] And while topics dear to theologians—such as the manner of divine activity and the survival of intelligence and life in the far future of the universe—remain largely absent from the purview of the physical sciences, there are important signs that a shift of perspective is underway.

This chapter examines certain knowns and unknowns discussed in Chapter Two, but from a theological viewpoint, through the lens of criteria that differ from scientific objectivism and its epistemological iteration, methodological naturalism. It also endeavours to show that despite this difference, at least in part, the Orthodox worldview matches trends and ideas in contemporary cosmology. Before anything else, however, and to pave the way for this book's fourth chapter, we present Orthodox theology as traditionally open to science, including cosmological ideas.

Should Orthodox Theology Be Afraid of Cosmology?

It has been observed that at the dawn of modern cosmology, believers as well as unbelievers experienced a shock. It all began with Copernicus and his successors, who displaced the earth from the centre and located it among the planets, with the final blow coming from the idea of the infinite universe, itself deprived of any centre. The contours of the traditional, hierarchically ordered, geocentric, and anthropocentric world vanished at the Copernican Turn of modern cosmology. The universe—understood as an objective quantity, an expanse of unfathomable size—was devoid of existential geodesics, meaningful symbols, and purposefulness. It was no longer able to shelter traditional values, qualitative assessments, and subjective approaches to reality. René Descartes represented this new worldview by his famed duality of *res cogitans* and *res extensa*, or mind and space, the former being seen as pure, immaterial subjectivity and the latter as inflexible, pointless objectivity.[17] But the early modern idea of a meaningless universe derived from an older theological assumption become influential before anyone had a chance to realise the implications of cosmic infinity.

Thus, a century before Descartes, Reformation theologians proclaimed the unique authority of Scripture (*sola scriptura*) in terms of communicating divine messages, which inadvertently led to the conclusion of a theologically meaningless universe. This caused a break in the long tradition of nature contemplation that viewed the cosmos as "another scripture" in which God's words could be read. This tradition originated in Scripture itself[18] and was well represented in the early Christian centuries.[19] It is the new *sola scriptura* theology that stripped the cosmos of theological significance, initiating the cultural process that—especially through Descartes' services—rendered it the exclusive province of quantitative assessments.[20] It did so, more specifically, by causing a rift between Christian thinking and philosophy, on the one hand, and the natural sciences, on the other hand, between qualitative and quantitative assessments. This break facilitated the turning of the tables on theology and metaphysics, whose dominance was soon after superseded by positivist science and methodological naturalism. Immediately relevant here is that this break paved the way for the representation of the cosmos as mute and meaningless in modern cosmology, which then caused an existential crisis with profound consequences. The ripples of this crisis endure.[21]

Against this changed theological landscape in the West, the impact of the emerging cosmology of an infinite universe was felt immediately. Blaise Pascal referred to "the infinite immensity of the spaces I ignore and that ignore me"[22] as the cause of this shock. (Mark the "I" of the philosophical approach to reality, an echo of Augustine's way of measuring the time.) It was the realisation of "an infinite sphere whose centre is everywhere and whose circumference is nowhere."[23] Subjective perceptions and the cosmos stopped being relevant to one another. Hence Pascal's admission on behalf of his generation of believers and unbelievers alike, "the eternal silence of these infinite spaces frightens me."[24] This universe was far remote from Clement's sense of the divine song reverberating "from centres to boundaries and from extremities to things in the middle," which structured reality.[25] It was C. S. Lewis' "silent planet,"[26] generalised for the cosmic scale, deprived of meaning and purpose—*tabula rasa*, an epistemological vacuum—and wholly antithetical to the "Great Dance" of all beings understood as singing centres within a meaningful universe.[27] This expanse was pointless and mute. (Not so the universe of contemporary cosmology that "hums" a tune of which scientists have become aware only very recently, which they are yet to decipher.)[28]

Within this infinite, open, uncentered, silent, and pointless universe—historians of science tell us—to affirm things like God's existence, personal emotions and insights, wisdom and values, and anthropocentric ideas was extremely difficult, if not outright impossible.[29] This terrible news caused dismay to many, much the way the West was disappointed when, at the daybreak of the second Christian millennium, the Lord's glorious return, expected to occur around the year 1000, literally, did not happen.[30] What matters is that cosmology became the enemy of many, believers and unbelievers alike. No wonder there was a stubborn commitment of various Christian quarters, including parts of Orthodox Christianity in the nineteenth century, to the Aristotelian cosmos, as Vasilios Makrides discusses.[31] Aristotle's cosmography (see Figure 3.2) supported the familiar ontological and axiological hierarchies that modern cosmology annulled.

Contemporary cosmology, with its billions of years of evolution, black holes, wormholes, dark matter, dark energy, and the multiverse, appears to impact people similarly, believers in particular—at least in the eyes of faith's antagonists who claim that there is neither room for nor evidence of God in

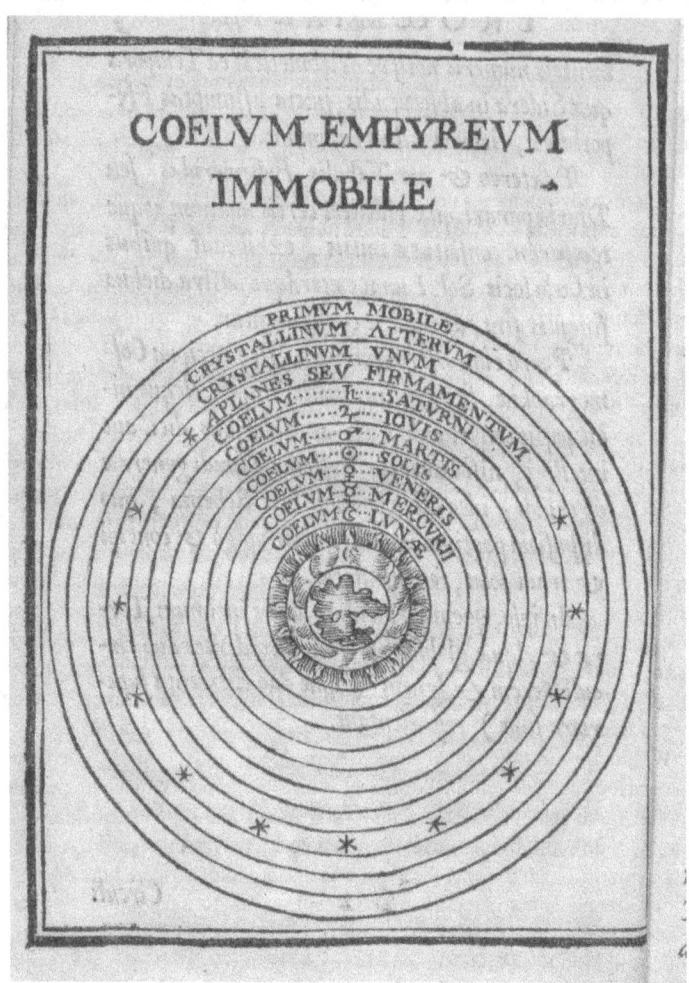

Figure 3.2 Christian Aristotelian Cosmography. The image shows page 4 of Pierre Gassendi's *Institutio astronomica* ("Astronomical instruction"; London, 1653), a work where the author reviews existing astronomical theories and presents his own discoveries. The edition also includes Galileo Galilei's *Sidereus nuncius* and Johannes Kepler's *Dioptrice*, important works of telescopic astronomy. The geocentric view of the cosmos shown here served as an axiological platform for ancient and medieval values.[32]

the universe as science knows it.³³ This kind of pronouncement is not unexpected, being consistent with methodological naturalism. To paraphrase Frank Nicholas, science is science, not theology.³⁴ The pronouncement that methodological naturalism has nothing to say about God could be contested only if it introduces itself as a theological and metaphysical statement outside of the purview of science, which sometimes happens.

Overall, contemporary Orthodox "apologists" miss this nuance and accordingly oppose cosmology and the natural sciences wholesale, chanting of the young and flat earth against the backdrop of a geocentric cosmos reduced to the size of the solar system in the name of "scientific" creationism.³⁵ They recycle premodern ideas about reality, which they combine with an understanding of divine activity as disruptive of the natural laws. But their "god-of-the-gaps," who lurks in the cracks and the clefts of the scientific narrative, and the "interventionist god," who disregards the natural laws, leave scientific matters unaddressed and are inconsistent with the Orthodox worldview.³⁶ The early Christians, indeed, whose wisdom the Orthodox tradition cherishes, were not interested in the age of the universe. It is true that the earliest known example relevant here, Clement of Alexandria, counted the years based on Genesis but did so for the purposes of establishing the chronology of a believing community, not to find out how old the cosmos could be.³⁷ A wide chasm separates the "apologetic" discourse and the Orthodox scholarship mentioned in the introduction to this book, including iterations of Orthodox natural theology.³⁸ The "apologetic" resistance to contemporary cosmology is not without consequences. It confirms the suspicion of the opposite side that Orthodox believers are incapacitated by the natural sciences—corresponding to the way less advanced cultures used to react to phenomena such as eclipses, while scientists study the heavens with utmost serenity (see Figure 3.3). In short, faith, including the Orthodox theology of creation, appears to believers and to scientifically minded people alike as unable to engage contemporary cosmology in a constructive fashion. That is not the case, however, at least when it comes to mature articulations of the Orthodox worldview.

For example, John Meyendorff praises a classic of the early Christian tradition, Basil of Caesarea, who, by affirming creation in time, not at once, advocated "the reality of a created movement and dynamism in creatures." Created beings, Meyendorff continues, "do not simply receive their form and diversity from God; they possess an energy, certainly also God-given, but authentically their own."³⁹ No nature-suppressing "interventionist god" here. Meyendorff interprets Basil's stance as naturalistic, setting a precedent for the incorporation of scientific information into the Orthodox representation of reality. If this assessment is accurate, and we have reasons to believe that it is (especially when it is understood in terms of the principle of synergy, to which we shall return),⁴⁰ the stance of the "apologists" is inconsistent with the Orthodox tradition. Their position shows an unwillingness to renounce

42 *What We Know and What We Don't Know about the Universe*

Figure 3.3 Jesuit Astronomers and the Siamese Populace. The image shows item 26 on page 230 of Guy Tachard's *A relation of the voyage to Siam performed by six Jesuits, sent by the French King, to the Indies and China, in the year, 1685* (London, 1688). It presents in contradistinction the Jesuit astronomers equipped with lunettes and the locals frightened by a lunar eclipse.[41]

the antiquated science and wrong theological ideas of ages past—including the "interventionist god" that acts sovereignly upon a passive, young cosmos created several millennia ago just the way we see it today.

Meyendorff is not the only Orthodox thinker of his generation able to identify patristic voices that tell a different story from the modern "apologetic" discourse—a story that matches Davison's concept of "imaginative apologetics," informed, rational, and engaged.[42] To give another example, after reviewing a wealth of patristic sources,[43] Lossky makes the useful point that to understand the early Christian worldview, believers need to translate its fundamental elements into the language of contemporary scientific culture. Such an undertaking would not defy the tradition; it would mark a return to it. In his words, to elaborate a comprehensive picture of reality, early theologians engaged "the conception of the universe which prevailed in their own age."[44] They did not consider ancient knowledge perfect and unchangeable, suitable for a "doctrinal synthesis" meant to endure forever. After all, Lossky continues, Christianity has "no philosophical preferences" and "freely makes use of philosophy and the sciences for apologetic purposes."[45] Here, "apologetic" means redrafting the Orthodox worldview within the parameters of any given culture. This amounts to another way of pursuing the goals of science-engaged theology. Lossky further points out that, theologically speaking, the early Christian worldview was unaffected by the ancient sciences employed for communicating its message.[46]

The early Christian approach corresponds to a method that can be useful to contemporary believers too, Lossky asserts within the same context, especially when it comes to science-engaged theology, as we would say today. As the ancient sciences did not affect the theological nature of the Orthodox worldview, he comments, contemporary sciences cannot do that either. And, to reach contemporary audiences, it is the sciences of today that should serve as a backdrop for the theological discourse, not ancient ideas of the cosmos.[47] Lossky's views echo Newman's.[48] Lossky himself illustrates this approach by acknowledging that the universe increases in complexity by virtue of its evolutionary dynamism.[49] His point is only tentative. That said, while he does not delve into this matter, the reader cannot miss that he alludes to the modern cosmological idea of the universe in expansion. So does, too, Stăniloae, by developing Lossky's intuitions into a system of theological cosmology articulated in the parameters of the evolutionary paradigm.[50] As we know from the introduction, the same goes for Nesteruk, who progressed beyond Stăniloae's theological integration of modern cosmology. To various degrees, the same goes for Theodosius Dobzhansky, Andrew Louth, and Panayiotis Nellas about evolutionary biology and anthropology.[51] In the same vein, elsewhere, Louth proposed that we read Maximus the Confessor's ideas about humankind and the cosmos not only within their historical context but as he would have presented them in our time.[52]

Equally useful is Lossky's point that Christians do not have to worry about new cosmological ideas, as their primary focus is salvation, not a certain description of the universe.[53] This point appears to mark a step back from the flexible view articulated earlier. However, the reader should be aware of the fact that Lossky had to grapple with the resistance of the "apologetic" discourse described above. Truth be told, most theologians of his generation were faced with the same reactionary mentality—and he was among the first Orthodox thinkers to challenge that narrative. No wonder he adopted a pastoral tone that, incidentally, corresponded to the approach of patristic theologians.[54] To return to the point about salvation, it is a step back only at face value. When this point is considered more closely, it is consistent with Lossky's idea of a theological worldview independent from science, yet a science that believers should embrace, not fear. It is on this note that we proceed to reflect upon what contemporary cosmology knows and ignores about the universe, theologically speaking.

Cosmology and Traditional Wisdom

In the face of scientific narratives such as that outlined in Chapter Two, we must return to one of Lossky's points discussed just above. We therefore ask: Does contemporary cosmology challenge the Orthodox Christian representation of reality? The response to this question cannot claim general acceptance. Not all Orthodox believers, whether theologically trained or not, uphold the same worldview. What is common sense for some is outrageous for others. Here, accordingly, we shall not discuss the concerns of believers who profess views of reality that differ from what seems to be the consensus of many illustrious Christian thinkers of the past, whose contributions set the foundations of Orthodox theology. But we hope that the ensuing comments will interest at least the readers who grasp the spirit of the tradition and who are committed to a comprehensive worldview, in patristic fashion, rather than "apologetic," partial, and reductionist surveys of the landscape. We also hope that the evidence presented in what follows will give scientifically informed readers a sense that Orthodox theology could be an interesting partner of conversation.

Keeping in mind the above, our short answer to the question is negative. We subscribe to Lossky's assessment of the situation. There is nothing to fear about contemporary cosmology, with its inability to gauge the universe's beginning, the perspective of a cosmos that continues to evolve and change since billions of years ago, the fact that the universe is swayed by elusive factors such as dark matter and dark energy, or, finally, that its expansion appears to wind down, causing the world to cease to be one day.[55] Believers, theologically trained or otherwise, should remember that their late ancient and medieval precursors—whose wisdom they hold dear and on which, for that reason, we build our argument—were eclectic about their sources and considered the cosmos from diverse viewpoints. Anchored in the normative doctrine of creation enshrined in the Nicene Creed—a doctrine that is schematic and therefore leaves ample room for development—the revered theologians of the past engaged various descriptions of reality without feeling discomforted by the available knowledge.[56] But, in so doing, they confessed incapacity to exhaust the mystery of a universe that, by and large, remains incomprehensible and ineffable. Lossky's apophatic attitude in regard to the cosmos echoes theirs. The examples that follow perfectly illustrate this view.

Noteworthy is Basil's stance, who considered the topic of the universe's beginning from various angles—pointing out that the polysemic word *beginning* "agrees with all its meanings" when it comes to the origin of the universe—and who concluded by expressing the impossibility to grasp all its implications.[57] No dramas, then, regardless of what scientific cosmology currently says or might one day say about the universe's beginning, the many worlds, the multiverse, and the far future.[58] The tradition prepares believers for many possibilities. Take Origen of Alexandria, for instance, who was adamant that, "according to the rule of faith," other worlds preceded this one: "Just as after the dissolution of this world will be another one, so also we believe others to have existed before this one was."[59] Basil seems to have corroborated this view when he observed that God's power cannot be limited to the creation of one world.[60] We leave out for now the topic of the creation of the universe and the universe's connection to the divine, but we shall return to it. Suffice it to point out here that for Orthodox believers any form of existence—from the large scale of the universe to the smallest grains of material accretion and quanta of energy and binary digits of information—is inconceivable without the ongoing divine input. As the Psalmist has it,

> All look to you to give them food in due season; when you give to them, they will gather, and when you open your hand, all things together will be filled with kindness. But when you turn away your face, they will be dismayed; you cancel their spirit, and they will fail and return to their dust. You will send forth your spirit, and they will be created, and you will renew the face of the ground.[61]

Paul concurs when he refers to the divine context of the universe's existence: "In him [namely, God] we live and move and have our being."[62] In Teilhard de Chardin's words, "God reveals himself everywhere . . . *as a universal milieu*, only because he is *the ultimate point* upon which all realities converge."[63]

It goes the same for cosmic evolution and change. That the universe is in constant movement and transformation should not bother Orthodox believers in the least. Having a beginning of its existence, the universe cannot be forever, nor can it be unmoved, nor can it reach ontological perfection. In Basil's words, again, "It is absolutely necessary that things begun in time also reach an end in time. If they have a beginning in time, do no doubt about their end."[64] And since temporality and finitude are intrinsic to their nature, all things experience change much the way time does. For Basil,

> The passage of time, which, together with the animals and plants within it, shares in the nature of the cosmos, always presses on and passes by . . . The same also is the nature of all the things that become, whether growing or decaying in whatever ways, which obviously are neither in a steady state nor possess immutability. Therefore, suitably, since they are enveloped in the nature of time—which shares in the nature of things that change—the bodies of animals and plants are necessarily bound by a sort of flowing condition, being moved to generation and corruption.[65]

Constant movement means neither stability nor unchangeability. Instability means imperfection. Perfection, whatever that might mean for the universe, pertains to the age to come, when the fundamental elements and the cosmos in its entirety will be reconfigured differently from the current shape of things. This is the teaching of the Scriptures[66] and the view of traditional witnesses such as Maximus the Confessor and Symeon the New Theologian. Maximus, for example, understands the eschatological event of resurrection as a transformation of both humankind and the cosmos. In his words, "the body will become like the soul and things material like things spiritual."[67] In the same vein, Symeon explains:

> Thus renewed, [the universe] will not return to what it had become in the beginning ... As the resurrected body of our Master and God was far different from the first [namely, Adam's body], so the creation in its entirety—in the same way and at the divine sign—will not return to what it was before, material and perceptible, but will be transformed by way of rebirth into an immaterial and spiritual dwelling, above what the senses can perceive.[68]

The universe will undergo a profound transformation at the eschaton, without analogy in either our current experience or in the history of the creation. Its only signposts are Christ's resurrected body and, we would add, altered physiological states experienced by certain saints. We shall return to this matter at the conclusion of the present chapter. This resurrectional state, for want of a better word, pertains to a physics of immortality whose properties escape both theology and the natural sciences. And until the universe reaches that state, cosmic evolution and the movement of everything within it will continue to entail alteration, death, and transformation.

Another point of interest is the contemporary view that the universe's history has already taken and will still take staggering eons. This is old news for Orthodox theologians, though the numbers of which we are aware could not have been known in the past. Even so, and putting aside Origen's successive worlds, according to the Orthodox tradition the cosmos was not made in one week, seven thousand years ago.[69] Its lifespan expands for seven or eight *ages* of indefinite lengths. Such is the belief of Bede the Venerable, John Damascene, and, again, Symeon's. Thus, Bede states that "the order of those six or seven days [of Genesis 1–2] in which it was created is also in harmony with the same number of its ages."[70] John similarly mentions that "this world supposedly has seven ages, namely, from the making of heaven and earth until the general consummation and resurrection."[71] In turn, Symeon explains that God "established the seven days as a type of the seven ages which would come later, and paradise he planted afterwards as a sign to the age to come."[72] His eschatological projection of the Genesis narrative of creation echoes Basil's take on Genesis 1:1 as a proleptic reference to creation's future transformation.[73] The early Christians and their medieval progeny were not scared by the perspective of a long history of the universe, which, we now know, counts billions of years. Nor were they hoping for the best of all possible worlds *before* the eschatological age.[74]

Throughout this unfathomable stretch of time, the universe undertakes countless changes, which Maximus calls inflations and deflations.[75] Change denotes imperfection. But more important is the traditional idea that change—indeed, evolution—is part and parcel of the creation's natural march through the ages. Much earlier, Gregory of Nyssa believed that the single event of creation in Genesis 1:1, so perceived contemplatively, unfolded as multiple events by which the original burst of energy called "light" or "fire" cooled down into the intricate cosmic patterns we still observe. In his words, "up to then [namely, the divine command of Genesis 1:3], light was gathered within itself, coextensive with the whole, but after [the commandment] it diversified into what was shared and what was distinct."[76] One could be tempted to see, here, a foreshadowing of the Big Bang theory and the universe's expansion of contemporary cosmology. And this is not the only place where Gregory articulates this view. He also shows that while the incipit of Genesis "mentions the fact that [God] created all of the beings, the [scriptural] discourse resolved to display the generation of each being distinctly, by a natural order of sorts."[77] The scriptural narrative does not account rigorously for how things occurred in past ages; it shows that things did not emerge simultaneously in a supernaturalist fashion. All phenomena within the universe follow the order of nature. Against this backdrop, of which he was perfectly aware, Stăniloae experienced no difficulty in agreeing to the current scientific description of the universe's evolution. He believed, for example, that by moving in time nature is dynamic, fertile, and efficient.[78] The same goes for contemporary Orthodox scholars such as Knight and Nesteruk.[79]

Turning to the view that the universe as we know it will one day cease to exist, it should not take the Orthodox by surprise either. They believe that the universe depends upon God in order to be and to thrive. Natural immortality is not an ontological given of the created cosmos.[80] As Athanasius of Alexandria shows, "when considered in itself, the nature of things that are being brought into existence (that is, which have their existence out of nonbeing) is fluid, weak, and mortal,"[81] or "fluid and dissolvable."[82] And he showed within the same context that all things depend on the Logos' providential activity. We already know that Basil subscribed to this understanding, saying: "It is absolutely necessary that things begun in time also reach an end in time."[83] Elsewhere, Basil addressed the creation's natural mortality from the angle of its composite structure. In his words,

> This very world is mortal and a place of mortals. Given that the constitution of things visible is complex and that all composite things must dissolve, they who are in the world and a part of the world necessarily share in the universe's nature.[84]

Biological and cosmic mortality are physical facts, whether understood as outcomes of the universe having a beginning or as caused by the composite nature of things. But, the early Christians were not pessimistic about the future. They believed that God's energy sustains all things in existence and that even though the universe will die one day, as humankind will, resurrection and transformation are what await the whole of the creation. We have seen previously several expressions of this conviction.

It follows that what the scientists currently know about the universe cannot shock Orthodox theologians and believers, at least not in regard to the traditional sources surveyed here. Granted, the Orthodox tradition does not provide us with the numbers, whether big or small, of the universe. After all, as Teilhard has it, "what ancient Thought glimpsed and imagined as natural harmony of Numbers, modern Science captured and clarified through the rigour of formulae grounded in Measure."[85] But even if the tradition does that—for instance, Gregory Palamas was interested in measuring the earth and in "natural knowledge" more broadly,[86] while Clement repeatedly referred to the numbers and the measures undergirding reality[87]—this is not what faith is about. Faith does not describe the universe, with its parameters and all that it contains; it interprets everything as creation, theologically, and affirms the indissoluble connection between God and all things.[88] But, before we turn to this connection, one more point is in order about the "dark side" of the universe and the significance of such terms as dark matter and dark energy for the Orthodox engagement of contemporary cosmology.

The Dark Side of Things and Divine Activity

The scientific narrative outlined in Chapter Two reaches the climax—at least in what concerns our topic—when it discusses the metaphorical "dark side" of the cosmos. We have seen above that this phrase denotes a humble approach to reality, an acknowledgment of the limitations of contemporary science. It signifies that cosmologists have stumbled upon a level of reality whose nature they cannot identify, that eludes observation and does not fit in the current models. This acknowledgment of limitations is of crucial importance for our scientific culture. Gone are the certainties of the nineteenth century, or even of the generation before our own, when optimistic researchers triumphantly announced that total knowledge is at hand, right behind the next corner. Step by step, relativity and quantum physics have cracked the walls of triumphalism, and so, too, did chaos theory, (the now almost extinct) string theory, M-theory, quantum gravity, the quest for the Theory of Everything, and other exotic items within the contemporary cosmological portfolio.[89] Limitations are equally obvious, we learnt in Chapter Two, in relation to not knowing where the universe comes from, why it is the way it is, and what the future holds in store for it.[90] The final blow to the culture of certainty and confidence came, however, from the discovery of what scientists had to designate as "dark," that is, unobservable and incomprehensible. And while we could expect the light to shine within this darkness at some point, sooner or later, what matters is the turning point the current impasse represents.

The clearest sign of a change of attitude in regard to what we know about the universe is, once again, the use of such enigmatic phrases as "dark matter" and "dark energy" that "carry with [them] a sufficient air of mystery," as Roger Penrose has it.[91] When contemporary cosmologists employ words such as these, what they mean is that they cannot grasp vast swathes of reality, its deeper, infrastructural levels. The previous chapter has informed us that seventy per cent of the universe must be dark energy, to which we should add twenty-five per cent dark matter, with all the stars, gas, planets, lifeforms, and people making five per cent of the whole. If these calculations are correct, ninety-five per cent of the universe escapes us. We know so much about the five per cent—though recent discoveries, such as the universe's "hum," mentioned earlier, show that our grasp of things is far from definitive—but are at a loss when it comes to most of the cosmos, its inner workings, or *le dedans des choses*, as Teilhard has it.[92] Our knowledge has led us to realise the immensity of the unknown. In Nesteruk's words,

> On the one hand cosmology provides us with a comprehensive theory of the universe supported by observations. On the other hand it has to admit that those forms of matter in the universe which are physically understood constitute only 4 percent of its material content (the remaining 96 percent associated with the so-called dark mass and dark energy remain as of yet beyond the reach of experiments; their existence is a matter of theoretical conviction).[93]

The one per cent difference between the estimation of Nesteruk and our own is of no concern here. What matters is that both views agree that most of nature eludes the current scientific models and observations. This is an admission of ignorance, though not of surrender, of course, as the quest for understanding continues. Theologically and spiritually speaking, it is an apophatic, humble attitude, the point where the triumphalist claim that has mobilised the scientific endeavour from the dawn of modernity breaks down. We already know from the previous chapter that the imperviousness of the "dark side" to our science means that we might need a new physics, which could possibly entail an entirely new perception of reality.[94] This is a wonderful moment in history. Cosmology must be admired not only for what it has managed to find out so far and for what it will undoubtedly discover in the future but also for acknowledging its own limitations. This acknowledgment brings it close—unexpectedly so—to Orthodox theology's sense of cosmic mystery. Penrose already referred to "mystery" in regard to cosmology's recent realisations, as we saw previously. But this admission of limitations heralds a new era for culture and society beyond cosmology and theology. Working independently, Sarah Beattie and Marcello La Matina echo this conviction, inviting a subtler and more comprehensive view of reality, near and far.[95] The same goes for a very recent article that explores the possibility of achieving meaningfulness and wellbeing through science.[96]

We wonder what the new perception of reality might be. There are voices out there, in the research and the thinking communities, that, as a counterpoint for the Cartesian division, call for bridging the mind, or consciousness, life more broadly, and the physical world.[97] The trailblazer of this view was Teilhard de Chardin. In his words,

> The moment has arrived for realising that, to be satisfactory, even a positivist interpretation of the Universe must include both the inside and the outside of things, Spirit and Matter at the same time. One day, true Physics will manage to integrate the whole Human into a coherent representation of the world.[98]

While the phrase "the whole Human" might raise eyebrows, given the idea behind it, that is, the universe aims towards humanisation, significant is Teilhard's view that the physics of the future should straddle the worlds that currently stand so far apart within our Cartesian culture, of spirit and matter or self and space. Without acknowledging Teilhard's pioneering contributions, Thomas Nagel captures this school of thought as follows:

> The existence of consciousness seems to imply that the physical description of the universe, in spite of its richness and explanatory power, is only part of the truth, and that the natural order is far less austere than it would be if physics and chemistry accounted for everything.[99]

It is likely that Nagel ignores Teilhard given the current view, also echoed by Sideris,[100] that his concept of "noosphere" would amount to a cumulative effect of human intellectual activities, which would not involve the world in its entirety. As we have seen above, this perception of Teilhard does not stand scrutiny; the "noosphere" is but the outburst of nature's inherent "psychism."

Either way, what Nagel proposes is the sense that the natural sciences of the future could recognise that "all the elements of the physical world are also mental."[101] Against this backdrop, the return to archaic ontologies such as panpsychism, where something akin to the "soul of the world" plays a central role,[102] should not come as a surprise. All this boils down to the perception that contemporary cosmology and certain traditional representations of reality are compatible and can intersect creatively. The idea is not new.

David Bohm and Fritjof Capra have already proved that such bridges are both possible and useful.[103] In turn, Werner Heisenberg and Michio Kaku showed that once we understand the meaning of their metaphors, we realise that certain ancient intuitions about reality foreshadow contemporary physics.[104] In the same vein, Basarab Nicolescu has declared bridging science and tradition a matter of urgency, proposing the "tridialectic" of the subject, the object, and their various encounters as the best way of reaching that goal.[105] Given the unfathomable extent of the unknown across the universe, proposals of this kind might gain further cultural weight. That contemporary cosmologists assiduously seek the Theory of Everything bodes well.[106] The same goes for the biologists who search for the bridge between physics and the emergence of life.[107]

It is at this juncture that the much-ridiculed "divine hypothesis," shunned by most natural scientists from the dawn of modernity to date, could be reconsidered. If a change of perception is at hand—corresponding to a new physics—then perhaps a change of dogma is in order, too, for the naturalist outlook of scientists, whether methodological or ontological, is not science. It is a reductionist model of reality, a dogmatic position, a philosophical conviction. What we propose is not a return to the "god-of-the-gaps" fallacy, even though the current lacunae in the scientific narrative greatly exceed what was discovered so far. We have no intention to plant the theological flag in the unfathomable blindspots of contemporary physics and cosmology. Our proposal does not need either the "god-of-the-gaps" or the "interventionist god" of the Western middle ages and early modernity—theological models that draw upon the metaphysical division of the natural and the supernatural orders of reality. Orthodox theology does not operate with this division. And it is this division that, together with *sola scriptura*, caused the modern clash between Christian theology and cosmology, or rather the wide array of natural sciences, eventually leading to the discredit of theology as competent for addressing matters of nature.

An explanation is in order. In short, medieval Western theology deployed the division between the natural and the supernatural levels of reality in order to assert the supernatural suspension of physical laws.[108] This division was a double-edged sword. The sciences, adopting methodological naturalism as their dogma, turned the tables on the medieval worldview by declaring supernatural agency redundant, given the completeness of nature and its perceived autonomy. Both sides played a zero-sum game, exploiting the medieval division after the either/or logic of the excluded middle. Thus, either the authority of theology and its supernaturalist explanations, drawing on belief, or the authority of science, with its naturalist explanation of phenomena, empirically substantiated by discovery and experiment. The current culture wars between theists and atheists and between creationists and evolutionists—whose symptom is the "apologetic" discourse earlier discussed—is not a new phenomenon. It is inherent to Western culture, originating in the dissociation between the natural and the supernatural.[109] As such, it is heterodox; foreign to the Orthodox tradition.

Orthodox theology works with different presuppositions. Specifically, the supernatural—a term that, in this case, denotes the divine activity in the world, not a layer of reality superposed to nature—is *within* the universe, not outside it. Nicholas' point that the "religious approach" locates God "at the heart of phenomena"[110] sums up perfectly its stance. The supernatural is inextricably mingled with nature's own matrix and energies.[111] Theologians and philosophers of all persuasions, including Orthodox ones, call this representation of reality "panentheism," which, briefly put, refers to God's presence in the universe and the universe's presence in God.[112] Panentheism and its corollary, the principle of synergy, are the preferred Orthodox way of representing reality, not contemporary panpsychism. We had an inkling of this model when we discussed Meyendorff's view of Basilian cosmology. Against this backdrop, God does neither disturb nor supersede the laws of nature. Nature's laws are the field where God operates *within* the cosmos as a "rationality" or an "underlying reality" irreducible to the material universe.[113] As such, what we call "nature" is synergy, the ground where the divine activity and the universe's own energies intersect and cooperate on an ongoing basis.[114] The classical early Christian locus of this synergetic aspect of reality is the prologue of John's Gospel, which emphasises the "work" of the Logos in the universe and the creation's response to the divine activity. Various early Christian theologians, such as Basil, Gregory of Nyssa, and John Chrysostom, were aware of the fundamental interaction between the divine and the cosmic energies.[115]

For example, metaphorically, Basil refers to nature's maternal, generative capacity that, divinely enhanced, becomes active and substantiates the patterns stowed within its bosom. In his words,

> Due to the latent potentiality stored in it by the demiurge, [matter] was in painful labour with the generation of all things, waiting for the auspicious times when, by a divine call, it would bring out into the open the things engendered within it.[116]

The same goes, Basil tells us, for other instances in the history of the universe, for example when, according to the Genesis creation narrative, plant life emerged from the earth:

> Let the earth bring forth! Think together with me how the cold and ever struggling [land] in the pangs of travail, being stirred up towards bearing fruit, at this small utterance and brief command produced myriads of sorts of plants.[117]

The land is not sterile; it experiences the pangs of childbearing. Its "coldness" denotes dependence on a range of factors when it comes to generating life, natural and supernatural alike. For theologians, the divine input is such a factor. No wonder the land reaches the point of giving birth at God's command understood as a supernatural energy that flows like blood through the veins of an eager body.

In like manner, but without using metaphors, Gregory repeatedly refers to God's "will, wisdom, and power" that underlie the natural processes at work within the universe, from the cosmos at large to atmospheric phenomena to the cycles of water within the earth's ecosphere.[118] As with Paul's divine milieu of the cosmos and life (see Acts 17:28, a passage central to panentheism), Gregory considers God the context of natural phenomena. In turn, on interpreting Genesis 1:2, John refers to the Spirit's interaction with the "waters" of the emerging universe:

> What is being meant by this [scriptural] utterance, namely, "the Spirit of God hovered over the water"? I am of the opinion that it means this, that a living energy of sorts was present in the waters. Water was not simply unmoved; it was both moving and endowed with a living power of sorts.[119]

As meaningful as Basil's metaphors are, John's discourse is even more apt at pointing out the double dynamic of nature, viewed as living or active "waters," and the Spirit who energises nature's potential, bringing it to the boiling point of its generative capacity. Irrespective of how they express this situation, all three authors agree that reality entails the interaction of various factors. For them, Genesis does not spell out a supernaturalist myth of origins that excludes natural processes. These authors viewed Genesis as telling the story of a continuous creation, an ongoing emergent phenomenon occurring in the parameters of a supernaturally enhanced nature, all through the history of the universe.[120]

The cosmological metaphors reviewed just above—bespeaking the latent generative quality of matter activated in the divine presence viewed as energy—do not constitute a rigorous formalisation of nature's algorithms but, we hope, should not be unintelligible to contemporary cosmologists. They are as suggestive as the Asian religious philosophies known to Bohm and Capra and perhaps less opaque than the scientists' "dark side" of reality. The universe these metaphors evoke is dynamic and evolving, in the making, bursting into being at the intersection of different forms of energy, be they dark or otherwise. If, for a moment, we put aside the divine input, this worldview fits the bill of contemporary cosmology to a tee, which perceives the cosmos as surfing the tides of an endless ocean of unknown energy. But the solution that originates in the patristic consensus on nature as an open field for the continuous interaction of divine and cosmic factors is equally important. Not abiding by the logic of either/or, this model works without the opposition of natural and supernatural agencies. God is *in* the universe, too, not only free of it, and interacts continuously with its infrastructure.[121] God's ongoing activity is part and parcel of what we call "nature." And, as in the prologue of John's Gospel, since the divine energy operates within the universe as the agency of the Logos, "nature" is also imbued with meaningfulness—for the Logos prints wisdom, the *logoi* or divine thoughts, in the matrix of all things.[122] To this matter we shall return in Chapter Four, in relation to the topic of nature contemplation. For now, suffice it to point out the difference between this perception of reality and the *sola scriptura* approach of Western theologians.

This way of representing reality differs from the Western opposition between the natural and the supernatural orders.[123] It appears to be gesturing towards the new physics contemporary scientists and philosophers are seeking or, as Teilhard would have it, *une science intégrale de la Nature* able to recognise the universal convergence of spiritual or psychic and material or physical energies.[124] As such, the worldview that emerges from the patristic consensus can coexist and creatively interact with the current—and indeed any other—cosmology. It requires neither the change of Orthodox theological worldview, with its emphasis on the divine energy at work in the universe's infrastructure, nor the rejection of science and the natural factors it studies. Lossky was right: Orthodox theology is equipped for engaging cosmology and the sciences more broadly. It is the task of this generation of theologians to determine whether the above are sufficient for developing Stăniloae's "theology of the world."

Open Questions

It is true that contemporary scientists, who represent nature as deprived of supernatural dimensions, for want of a better word, might consider the previous proposal with suspicion. Methodological naturalism imposes restrictions on them. And this short book does not mean to impose on them a theological view of reality. Except for the "apologists" of heterodox ideas, Orthodox theologians do not aspire to become "cosmic revolutionaries" who push the envelope of a mythical worldview *as* science.[125]

However, Orthodox theologians would hope that contemporary cosmologists, accustomed to having direct access only to four or five per cent of the universe, might be more open to strange new worlds than their predecessors were. Would the cosmologists of our age allow for the unthinkable and the unexpected, whatever the form these might take—especially since their universe is no longer made of pure and simple matter, the thick stuff the physics of a few centuries ago considered to be the ultimate reality? Would they embrace the New Copernican Turn? Knight, an astrophysicist turned Orthodox theologian, hinted at this possibility while he pondered divine activity as unfolding alongside and through nature's processes, with some of these processes eluding the grasp of science, perhaps forever.[126] To reject the "divine hypothesis" as proposed above—in the sense of an ongoing supernatural agency operating *within* the universe in harmonious conjunction with the latter's energies—before testing it would betray entrenched ideological commitments, not readiness to articulate the new physics.

The active God of the present proposal is not the old man hiding on the dark side of the moon—or over the rainbow—whence he throws wrathful thunderbolts at sinful earthlings, disturbing the order of nature at whim. It is, as Clement suggests, the "pure song" that reverberates to and fro in the background of the universe;[127] Gregory the Theologian's transcendent "fire" that permeates the cosmos, moving through all things and connecting them;[128] Basil's "divine words" that "run" through the nature of things to the end of time;[129] John Chrysostom's "living energy" of the Spirit that enlivens the "waters" (the fields? the waves?) of the universe;[130] and Maximus' "unifying force" that binds the cosmic regions together *from within* in the light of a divine blueprint of the creation.[131] In response, the saints perceive the cosmos divinely—as a diaphanous and luminous milieu, in the words of Diadochus of Photiki,[132] or unified as "a single ray of the sun," to use the phrase of Gregory the Great[133] and Adomnán of Iona,[134] or as compact as a hazelnut held in one's palm, as Julian of Norwich has it.[135] In the same vein, Stăniloae contemplates the universe as engaged on a "spiritual vertical, on a trajectory of spiritual convergence and towards the fuller assimilation of matter by the spirit."[136] Lossky captures this perception of reality in reference to the Christian mystics who experience "an ascent in the course of which the universe appears more and more unified, more and more coherent, penetrated with spiritual forces and forming one whole within the hand of God."[137] This theological worldview transcends the binary view of the natural and the supernatural orders as opposite ends of the ontological spectrum.

What becomes increasingly obvious, largely due to the advancement of hagiographical studies in conjunction with other disciplines, such as cognitive science,[138] is that this theological worldview is not quite as untestable as many contemporaries still think it is. While the divine omnipresent activity eludes both current cosmological and physical models, as well as the available measuring devices, it is not immaterial. Believers are convinced that they are not left without signs of the divine energy that works by default in the background of reality under the guise of providence.[139] But the interdisciplinary study of hagiography has recently yielded more clues, of which the transformed bodies of the saints that radiate dazzling light,[140] are as subtle as the air,[141] and able to levitate[142] seem to be its most tangible proofs. By refracting the glory of God's active presence on a recurrent basis throughout history—testing the theory through experiment, as it were, in many times and places—the transfigured bodies of the saints help us to "discover the universal underneath the exceptional," to paraphrase Teilhard's words.[143] These experiences of a "natural" order that includes the "supernatural" one are real and documented throughout history. They denote the existence of unknown physical laws, perhaps a physics of immortality, perhaps what contemporary scientists will find behind the curtain of the universe's "dark side."

It is very possible, furthermore, that the resplendent bodies of the saints, together with "miracles" or "signs,"[144] are not merely pointers to yet undiscovered natural laws. They appear to be proleptic models (after the scientific fashion) of the future state of things,[145] of laws that do not operate yet, allowing us to predict the shape of things to come. These bodies make present in the here and now a level of intimacy between God and nature that pertains to the future age—"a new heaven and a new earth" when God will be "all in all,"[146] when God and the universe will breathe together in one go.[147] It all sounds mythical, but does it? We are dwellers of a multiverse where nothing improbable is, of necessity, impossible. The miracles and the transfigured bodies of the saints might anticipate accelerated natural processes as they will unfold in the far future, for they are real, even though they do not belong in the here and now.

Would the physics of tomorrow be able to include what Orthodox theology calls the supernatural that permeates the natural continuum? Would it be able to accommodate the view that the future will bring with it the outcomes of the subtle process already at work, unbeknown to us, within the infrastructure of reality—or that a different set of laws of nature will operate in the far future of the universe, perhaps symmetrical to the laws of the earliest universe, which still elude us? Irrespective of how the cosmologists of tomorrow will respond to these questions, they can be certain of one thing, namely, Orthodox theology is not against science. We have seen previously that a plethora of modern and contemporary authors attest to this fact. For, traditionally, Orthodox theology has always incorporated scientific information as a starting point for its contemplation of God's creation, the universe.[148]

It is on this note that we draw the final line of this chapter, pointing out that—apart from its convictions regarding divine activity—what Orthodox theology doesn't know about the universe overlaps with what contemporary science knows and knows not about it. For the Orthodox theological worldview is not scientific, regardless of how much it would engage the sciences, including cosmology, at any given time in the course of its march through history. And so, what the cosmologists of tomorrow will discover about the universe will be as exciting for the Orthodox as it will be for themselves. We have come to know much, scientists and theologians alike, and in the foregoing we have learnt that much more awaits us out there. We must continue to wonder at the universe's vastness and complexity, seeking to grasp its marvels. The story of the self, to which we turn in what follows, is one such marvel.

Notes

1 While feedback and peer review have become staples of the humanities in modern times, subjectivity is still to be expected. See Marcello La Matina, "On Subjects, Objects, Transitional Fields, and Icons: The Semiotics of a New Paradigm in Human Studies," *Christian Perspectives on Science and Technology*, New Series, 1 (2022): 108–49, esp.

108–11; Andrew Louth, *Discerning the Mystery: An Essay on the Nature of Theology* (Oxford: Clarendon Press, 1989), xi–xiii, 1–72.
2 See on this the interesting discussion of Richard Rudner, "The Scientist Qua Scientist Makes Value Judgments," *Philosophy of Science* 20, no. 1 (1953): 1–6, https://doi.org/10.1086/287231, and Richard C. Jeffrey, "Valuation and Acceptance of Scientific Hypotheses," *Philosophy of Science* 23, no. 3 (1956): 237–46, https://doi.org/10.1086/287489. For a very recent take on the matter, see Heather Douglas, "The Importance of Values for Science," *Interdisciplinary Science Reviews* 48, no. 2 (2023): 251–63, https://doi.org/10.1080/03080188.2023.2191559.
3 See, for example, Maximus the Confessor, *Mystagogia* (hereafter, *The Mystagogy*), prologue.
4 See Knight, *Eastern Orthodoxy*, 16–21.
5 Credit: The University of Sydney Library's Rare Books and Special Collections. This is one of only four known copies that were sent by Newton and his assistant to other mathematicians in order to eliminate any errors in a second edition. Call number: Restricted Wing N1048, accessed 15 March 2024, https://tinyurl.com/y5wh8nya. The digitised version of the book is found at https://digital.library.sydney.edu.au/nodes/view/7454.
6 For notes to that effect, see the following contributions to *The Early Christian World*, 2nd ed. Philip F. Esler, Routledge Worlds (London and New York: Routledge, 2017): Piotr Ashwin-Siejkowski, "Creeds, Councils, Doctrinal Development," 631–46; Mark Edwards, "The Development of Office in the Early Church," 284–94; Thomas P. Scheck, "Origen," 943–58. See also Josef Lössl, "Tatian, Theophilus of Antioch and Irenaeus of Lyons," in *The Routledge Handbook of Early Christian Philosophy*, ed. Mark Edwards (London and New York: Routledge, 2021), 342–56. See also the following contributions to *The Cambridge History of Early Christian Literature*, ed. Frances Young, Lewis Ayres, and Andrew Louth (Cambridge: Cambridge University Press, 2004): Ronald E. Heine, "The Alexandrians," 117–30; Richard A. Norris, "Irenaeus of Lyon," 45–52; Richard A. Norris, "Articulating identity," 71–90; Frances Young, "Christian Teaching," 91–104.
7 See Richard A. Norris, "The Apostolic and Sub-Apostolic Writings: The New Testament and the Apostolic Fathers," in *The Cambridge History of Early Christian Literature*, ed. Frances Young, Lewis Ayres, and Andrew Louth (Cambridge: Cambridge University Press, 2004), 11–19.
8 Augustine, *Confessions* 11.27.36. Unless otherwise stated, all translations from classical and modern languages are by Costache.
9 Christos Yannaras, *Elements of Faith: An Introduction to Orthodox Theology*, trans. Keith Schram (Edinburgh: T&T Clark, 1991), 17. The word *apophatic* is of Greek origin and it literally means "restraint from talking" or "keeping quiet."
10 Vladimir Lossky, *The Mystical Theology of the Eastern Church* (Crestwood, NY: St Vladimir's Seminary Press, 2002), 91. For a recent iteration of this approach, see Nesteruk, *The Sense of the Universe*, 199–254.

11 Clement, *Stromateis* 5.11.73.2–3; 6.8.68.2; 6.8.70.2; John Chrysostom, *Homilies on Genesis* 2.5. See Costache, *Humankind and the Cosmos*, 133–35.
12 Pierre Teilhard de Chardin, *Le phénomène humain* (Paris: Seuil, 1956), 49–50.
13 Tyson, "Learned Ignorance?" 2–3.
14 See Roger Wagner and Andrew Briggs, *The Penultimate Curiosity: How Science Swims in the Slipstream of Ultimate Questions* (Oxford: Oxford University Press, 2016), 304–10.
15 Newman, *Scope and Nature*, 213.
16 Nesteruk, *The Sense of the Universe*, 32.
17 Descartes, *Discourse on the Method*, 4.
18 See Psalms 18:1–4 (New English Translation of the Septuagint; hereafter, NETS); Romans 1:19–20 (New Revised Standard Version; hereafter, NRSV).
19 See Paul M. Blowers, *Drama of the Divine Economy: Creator and Creation in Early Christian Theology and Piety* (Oxford: Oxford University Press, 2012), 315–35; Costache, *Humankind and the Cosmos*, 128–36, 153–60, 178–86, 270–78; Joshua Lollar, *To See into the Life of Things: The Contemplation of Nature in Maximus the Confessor and His Predecessors*, Monothéisme et philosophie (Turnhout: Brepols, 2013), 107–18.
20 For the chronology of this development within the Christian thought, see Peter Harrison, *The Bible, Protestantism, and the Rise of Natural Science* (Cambridge: Cambridge University Press, 1998). See also Harrison, *Territories*, 74–78, for the earlier process of depriving Scripture and the "book of nature" of their symbols through the abandonment of allegorical interpretation. His conclusions do not weaken our point about *sola scriptura* as a theological assumption of a meaningless universe.
21 Newman, *Scope and Nature*, 209, 215, 218; Walker Percy, *Lost in the Cosmos: The Last Self-Help Book* (New York: Open Road, 2011; ebook ed.; 1st ed., 1983), 173. For a succinct overview of this crisis, see Costache, "Theological Anthropology Today," 168–69.
22 Pascal, *Pensées*, 102.
23 Pascal, *Pensées*, 230.
24 Pascal, *Pensées*, 233.
25 Clement, *Le Protreptique* (hereafter, *Exhortation*) 1.5.2. See Costache, *Humankind and the Cosmos*, 91–94.
26 See C. S. Lewis, *Out of the Silent Planet* (ch. 18; ch. 20) and *Perelandra* (ch. 2), in *The Space Trilogy: Out of the Silent Planet—Perelandra—That Hideous Strength* (London: HarperCollins Publishers, 2013), 110–11, 119, 165.
27 Lewis, *Perelandra* (ch. 17), 334–39.
28 See Jonathan O'Callaghan, "A Background 'Hum' Pervades the Universe. Scientists Are Racing to Find Its Source," *Scientific American*, August 4, 2023, accessed August 20, 2023, http://tinyurl.com/mpm5f2py.

29 Alexandre Koyré, *From the Closed World to the Infinite Universe* (Baltimore, MD: The Johns Hopkins Press, 1957), 1–3, 273–76. See also, briefly, Lossky, *Mystical Theology*, 105.
30 Georges Duby, *L'An Mil*, Folio Histoire (Paris: Gallimard, 1980), 11–13, 283–84; Alexandru Mironescu, *Certitudine și adevăr* (certainty and truth) (București: Harisma, 1992), 27–28.
31 See Vasilios N. Makrides, "Orthodoxy Matters: Why Has a Scientific Revolution Not Taken Place in the Greek East?" in *Orthodox Christianity and Modern Science: Past, Present and Future* (2022): 15–44, esp. 27–42.
32 Credit: The University of Sydney Library's Rare Books and Special Collections. Call number: Deane Wing G291A, accessed March 20, 2024, https://tinyurl.com/y3698azs.
33 Stephen Hawking, *Brief Answers to Big Questions* (London: John Murray, 2018), 23–38.
34 See Frank W. Nicholas, "Religion's Openness Towards Science," *Nature* 546 (2017): 474.
35 For analyses of this kind of Orthodox discourse, see Christopher Howell, "The Rose and the Stag: An American Orthodox Conversation on Modernity, Science, and Biblical Interpretation," *Almagest* 9, no. 2 (2019): 40–59; Christopher C. Knight, "Natural Theology and the Eastern Orthodox Tradition," in *The Oxford Handbook of Natural Theology*, ed. Russell Re Manning (Oxford: Oxford University Press, 2013), 213–26, esp. 213, 224; Efthymios Nicolaidis, "Creationism in Today's Orthodox Community," *Almagest* 12 (2021): 208–27, https://doi.org/10.1484/J.ALMAGEST.5.125391.
36 See Costache, "The Orthodox Doctrine of Creation," 49–62; Andrew Davison, *Participation in God: A Study in Christian Doctrine and Metaphysics* (Cambridge: Cambridge University Press, 2019), 13–38.
37 See Clement, *Stromateis* 1.140.1–7.
38 Here are a few more relevant sources: David Bradshaw and Richard Swinburne, eds., *Natural Theology in the Eastern Orthodox Tradition* (St Paul, MN: IOTA Publications, 2021); Christopher K. Knight, *Science and the Christian Faith: A Guide for the Perplexed*, Foundations (Crestwood, NY: St Vladimir's Seminary Press, 2021); Christopher Knight, "Divine Action and the Laws of Nature: An Orthodox Perspective on Miracles," in *Science and the Eastern Orthodox Church*, ed. Daniel Buxhoeveden and Gayle Woloschak (London and New York: Routledge, 2016), 41–51; Christopher K. Knight, *The God of Nature: Incarnation and Contemporary Science*, Theology and the Sciences (Minneapolis, MN: Augsburg Fortress Publishers, 2007); Elizabeth Theokritoff and Christopher C. Knight, "Twentieth- and Twenty-First-Century Orthodox Voices on Nature and Science," in *The T&T Clark Handbook of Christian Theology and the Modern Sciences*, ed. John Slattery (Bloomsbury/T&T Clark, 2020), 177–90.
39 John Meyendorff, *Byzantine Theology: Historical Trends and Doctrinal Themes* (New York: Fordham University Press, 1979), 133. For the complexity of Basil's take on creation, see Andrew J. Brown, *Recruiting the*

Ancients for the Creation Debate (Grand Rapids, MI: Eerdmans, 2023), 127–48 (siding with Meyendorff, we take exception to the author's suggestion that Basil was a precursor of modern "young earth" creationism); Charlotte Köckert, *Christliche Kosmologie und kaiserzeitliche Philosophie: Die Auslegung des Schöpfungsberichtes bei Origenes, Basilius und Gregor von Nyssa vor dem Hintergrund kaiserzeitlicher Timaeus-Interpretationen*, Studien und Texte zu Antike und Christentum 56 (Tübingen: Mohr Siebeck, 2009), 312–98.

40 See Costache, *Humankind and the Cosmos*, 242–58 (these pages engage Meyendorff's assessment explicitly). For similar conclusions, drawn independently, see Knight, *Eastern Orthodoxy*, 40–47.

41 Credit: The University of Sydney Library's Rare Books and Special Collections. Call number: Wing T96, accessed 20 March 2024, https://tinyurl.com/y7uz875f.

42 Andrew Davison, "Introduction" to *Imaginative Apologetics: Theology, Philosophy and the Catholic Tradition* (London: SCM Press, 2011), xxv–xxvi.

43 Lossky, *Mystical Theology*, 91–113.

44 Lossky, *Mystical Theology*, 104. See Costache, *Humankind and the Cosmos*, 232–34.

45 Lossky, *Mystical Theology*, 104.

46 Ibid. See also Costache's notes in "Patristic and Neopatristic Antecedents," 138–42.

47 Lossky, *Mystical Theology*, 104–06.

48 Newman, *Scope and Nature*, 255.

49 Lossky, *Mystical Theology*, 241.

50 See Costache, "A Theology of the World," 208–12. See also Elizabeth Theokritoff, "Creator and Creation," in *The Cambridge Companion to Orthodox Christian Theology*, ed. Mary B. Cunningham and Elizabeth Theokritoff (Cambridge: Cambridge University Press, 2008), 63–77, esp. 68–69.

51 Christopher Howell, "Between Darwin and Dostoevsky: The Syntheses of Theodosius Dobzhansky," *Christian Perspectives on Science and Technology*, New Series 1 (2022): 28–45; Andrew Louth, *Introducing Eastern Orthodox Theology* (Downers Grove, IL: IVP Academic, 2013), 74–78; Nellas, *Deification in Christ*, 33, 41–42.

52 Andrew Louth, "Man and Cosmos in St. Maximus the Confessor," in *Toward an Ecology of Transfiguration*, ed. John Chryssavgis and Bruce V. Foltz, Orthodox Christianity and Contemporary Thought (New York: Fordham University Press, 2013), 59–71. His approach echoes Staniloae's in *Teologia dogmatică ortodoxă*, 1: 6.

53 Lossky, *Mystical Theology*, 105.

54 For the pastoral underpinnings of the patristic discourse on the cosmos, see Costache, *Humankind and the Cosmos*, 13, 19, 61, 223–25, 233, 266–67, 280, 281, 285.

55 See Lewis and Barnes, *A Fortunate Universe*, 129–81.

56 See Costache, "The Orthodox Doctrine of Creation," 49; Lossky, *Mystical Theology*, 104–06.

57 *Homélies sur l'hexaéméron* (hereafter, *Homilies on the Hexaemeron*) 1.2–3, 5–6. For recent studies of Basil's approach to this topic, see Brown, *Recruiting the Ancients*, 140–45; Costache, *Humankind and the Cosmos*, 231–34, 239–40. Brown and Costache's assessments differ, with the former presenting Basil as a literal reader of Genesis 1, while the latter bringing to light Basil's nuanced thinking.

58 Already Hawking suggested the possibility of understanding the current state of the universe without needing a beginning. Hawking, *A Brief History of Time*, 141–44. His views on this matter fluctuated over time. See Robert P. Crease, "The Never-Ending Quest for a Beginning," *Nature* 616 (2023): 243–44, https://doi.org/10.1038/d41586-023-00977-3.

59 Origen, *On First Principles* 3.5.3. He returned time and again to this idea. See *On First Principles* 2.3.1; 2.3.4; 2.3.5. See Costache, *Humankind and the Cosmos*, 88.

60 See Basil's reference to "the maker of this universe, whose creative power is not limited to one world, but infinitely exceeds it" (*Homilies on the Hexaemeron* 1.2). As a parallel over the gulfs of history, John Wesley, who was an avid reader of patristic works, did not reject the possibility of other (inhabited) worlds but claimed ignorance about such worlds. See O'Brien, "John Wesley's Theological Anthropology," 21.

61 Psalms 103:27–30 (NETS).

62 Acts 17:28 (NRSV).

63 Pierre Teilhard de Chardin, *Le Milieu Divin: An Essay on the Interior Life* (London: Collins, 1962), 113–14.

64 Basil, *Homilies on the Hexaemeron* 1.3. See Lossky, *Mystical Theology*, 93.

65 Basil, *Homilies on the Hexaemeron* 1.5. Basil's brother, Gregory of Nyssa, was of the same view. See the recent analysis of his views by Isidoros C. Katsos, *The Metaphysics of Light in the Hexaemeral Literature: From Philo of Alexandria to Gregory of Nyssa* (Oxford: Oxford University Press, 2023), 91–96.

66 See 2 Peter 3:10–13; Revelation 21:1.

67 Maximus, *The Mystagogy* 7.

68 Symeon, *Ethical Discourses* 1.5.

69 For a recent survey of the topic, see Brown, *Recruiting the Ancients*, 23–183.

70 Bede, *Commentary on the Beginning of Genesis* 1.35–36. For a different understanding of Bede's approach, see Brown, *Recruiting the Ancients*, 187–89.

71 John Damascene, *An Exact Exposition of the Orthodox Faith* 2.1. See Costache, "Maximus and John," 89–90 and "The Orthodox Doctrine of Creation," 52.

72 Symeon, *Ethical Discourses* 1.1.

73 "The statement by anticipation of the dogmas regarding the world's consummation and transformation is now handed on briefly by way of the fundamentals pertaining to the divinely inspired teaching: In the beginning God made" (Basil, *Homilies on the Hexaemeron* 1.3). For an analysis of this passage, see Costache, *Humankind and the Cosmos*, 239–40.

The idea of Genesis 1 as prophecy was widespread in the early Christian centuries. See Blowers, *Drama of the Divine Economy*, 103–05.

74 See Doru Costache, "Affirming Creation's Goodness in a Time of Pandemic: Patristic Insights," *Colloquium* 54, no. 2 (2022): 9–32, esp. 17–21.
75 Maximus, *On Difficulties in the Church Fathers* (hereafter, *Difficulties*) 10.89.1–5; 10.90.8–12; *Quaestiones ad Thalassium* (hereafter, *Answers to Thalassius*) 60. See Costache, "Maximus and John," 83.
76 Gregory of Nyssa, *In Hexaemeron* (hereafter, *An Apology for the Hexaemeron*), 65. See Costache, *Humankind and the Cosmos*, 316–26; Katsos, *The Metaphysics of Light*, 96–105.
77 Gregory of Nyssa, *An Apology for the Hexaemeron* 64.
78 See, e.g., Stăniloae, *Teologia dogmatică ortodoxă*, 1:339 and 2:7. See also Costache, "A Theology of the World," 209, 211–12, and the references therein.
79 Knight, *Eastern Orthodoxy*, 30 n.125, 38, 39, 46; Nesteruk, *The Sense of the Universe*, 9, 32, 79, 82, 106–07.
80 See Psalms 101:26–28 (NETS); Hebrews 1:10–12 (NRSV).
81 Athanasius, *Contra Gentes* (hereafter, *Against the Gentiles*) 41.
82 Athanasius, *Against the Gentiles* 41. See Costache, "The Orthodox Doctrine of Creation," 52, 55.
83 Basil, *Homilies on the Hexaemeron* 1.3.
84 Basil, *Homily on Psalm* 114.5.
85 Teilhard de Chardin, *Le phénomène humain*, 46.
86 Gregory Palamas, *One Hundred and Fifty Chapters* 1–33. See Doru Costache, "Queen of the Sciences? Theology and Natural Knowledge in St Gregory Palamas' *One Hundred and Fifty Chapters*," *Transdisciplinarity in Science and Religion* 3 (2008): 27–46, esp. 31–34.
87 Clement refers to the "measure and number of all things" in *Exhortation* 6.69.2. See Costache, *Humankind and the Cosmos*, 16, 92–93, 119–20, 125, 372.
88 See Doru Costache, "One Description, Multiple Interpretations: Suggesting a Way Out of the Current Impasse," in *Orthodox Christianity and Modern Sciences: Theological, Philosophical, Scientific and Historical Aspects of the Dialogue*, 33–49, esp. 35–37.
89 See Chris Ferrie and Geraint F. Lewis, *Where Did the Universe Come From? And Other Cosmic Questions: Our Universe, from the Quantum to the Cosmos* (Naperville, IL: Sourcebooks, 2021), 191–94, 201–207.
90 See John D. Barrow, *The Constants of Nature: From Alpha to Omega— The Numbers That Encode the Deepest Secrets of the Universe* (New York: Pantheon Books, 2002), 177–200, 275–92; Ferrie and Lewis, *Where Did the Universe Come From?* 21–37, 184–94; Lewis and Barnes, *A Fortunate Universe*, 182–236.
91 Roger Penrose, *The Road to Reality: A Complete Guide to the Laws of the Universe* (London: Jonathan Cape, 2004), 773, 777, 1023.
92 Teilhard de Chardin, *Le phénomène humain*, 49–54.
93 Nesteruk, *The Sense of the Universe*, 32.
94 See Ferrie and Lewis, *Where Did the Universe Come From?*, 217; Penrose, *The Road to Reality*, 18–19.

95 Sarah Ann Beattie, "From Eden to Interstellar Space: Thomas Nagel, Biblical Hermeneutics and the Search for 'the True Extent of Reality'" (PhD diss., University of Divinity, 2022), 80–95; La Matina, "On Subjects," 127–31, 135–41, 145–49.

96 See Jesse L. Preston, Thomas J. Coleman III, and Faith Shin, "Spirituality of Science: Implications for Meaning, Well-Being, and Learning," *Personality and Social Psychology Bulletin* (2023), https://doi.org/10.1177/01461672231191356.

97 Beattie, "From Eden to Interstellar Space," 23–32, 46–55; Penrose, *The Road to Reality*, 1029–33; Roger Penrose, *The Emperor's New Mind: Concerning Computers, Minds, and the Laws of Physics* (New York: Penguin Books, 1991), 405–50; Henry P. Stapp, *Mindful Universe: Quantum Mechanics and the Participating Observer*, 2nd ed. (Berlin and Heidelberg: Springer, 2011), 79–84, 119–37.

98 Teilhard de Chardin, *Le phénomène humain*, 30.

99 Thomas Nagel, *Mind and Cosmos: Why the Materialist Neo-Darwinian Conception of Nature Is Almost Certainly False* (New York: Oxford University Press, 2012), 35.

100 Sideris, "Religion," 907–08.

101 Nagel, *Mind and Cosmos*, 57.

102 Johann Leidenhag, *Minding Creation: Theological Panpsychism and the Doctrine of Creation*, T&T Clark Studies in Systematic Theology 37 (London: T&T Clark, 2021), 49–86.

103 David Bohm, *Wholeness and the Implicate Order* (London: Routledge, 1980); Fritjof Capra, *The Tao of Physics: An Exploration of the Parallels Between Modern Physics and Eastern Mysticism* (Boulder, CO: Shambala, 1975). Recently, one of us coauthored an article that explores the possibility of applying Bohm's approach to Eastern religious philosophies for the way Orthodox Christianity can interact with contemporary cosmology. See Grijs and Costache, "The Cosmology of David Bohm," 205, 210–16.

104 Werner Heisenberg, *Physics and Philosophy: The Revolution in Modern Science*, World Perspectives (London: George Allen & Unwin, 1971), 61; Michio Kaku, *Parallel Worlds: A Journey Through Creation, Higher Dimensions, and the Future of the Cosmos* (New York: Doubleday, 2006), 17–18, 196–98.

105 Basarab Nicolescu, *Nous, la particule et le monde*, 2nd ed. (Monaco: Éditions du Rocher, 2002), 177–240. For a similar intuition in regard to the humanities, see La Matina, "On Subjects," 127–31.

106 See Barrow, *The Constants of Nature*, 53–76; Stephen W. Hawking, *The Theory of Everything: The Origin and Fate of the Universe*, special anniversary ed. (Beverly Hills, CA: Phoenix Books, 2005), 119–36; Penrose, *The Road to Reality*, 627, 1010–11, 1028.

107 See George F. R. Ellis, "A Foundational View of the Physics of Evolution," *Nature* 622 (2023): 247–49, https://doi.org/10.1038/d41586-023-03061-y; Abhishek Sharma et al., "Assembly Theory Explains and Quantifies Selection and Evolution," *Nature* 622 (2023): 321–29, https://doi.org/10.1038/s41586-023-06600-9.

108 See Edward Grant, *A History of Natural Philosophy: From the Ancient World to the Nineteenth Century* (Cambridge: Cambridge University Press, 2007), 174, 201, 203, 223, 226, 250, 252, 255, 257, 262, 283, 291; Keith Hutchinson, "The Natural, the Supernatural, and the Occult in the Scholastic Universe," in *1543 and All That: Image and Word, Change and Continuity in the Proto-Scientific Revolution*, ed. Guy Freeland and Anthony Corones, Australasian Studies in History and Philosophy of Science 13 (Dordrecht: Springer Science+Business Media, 2000), 333–55.

109 Costache, *Humankind and the Cosmos*, 254–58; Knight, *Eastern Orthodoxy*, 47–51. There are exceptions, of course. In early modernity, despite this background, John Wesley was able to accommodate a model of the universe where God's power and the law of gravity worked hand-in-hand. See O'Brien, "John Wesley's Theological Anthropology," 15.

110 Nicholas, "Religion's Openness," 474.

111 Costache, *Humankind and the Cosmos*, 368–73; Davison, *Participation in God*, 217–18, 228–35; Nicola Hoggard Creegan, "A Christian Theology of Evolution and Participation," Zygon 42, no. 2 (2007): 499–518, esp. 509–16; Knight, *Eastern Orthodoxy*, 47–51; Knight, "Divine Action and the Laws of Nature," 44–46; Lossky, *Mystical Theology*, 88–89, 97–98; Louth, *Introducing Eastern Orthodox Theology*, 39–41; Meyendorff, *Byzantine Theology*, 2, 3, 76–78, 133–34; Stăniloae, *Teologia dogmatică ortodoxă*, 1: 346–47.

112 See Alexandros Batalias, "Emergentist Panentheism and Orthodox Theology: A Preliminary Encounter," *Theophany* 5 (2023): 45–77; Uwe Meixner, "Orthodox Panentheism: Sergius Bulgakov's Sophiology," in *Panentheism and Panpsychism: Philosophy of Religion meets Philosophy of Mind*, ed. Godehard Brüntrup, Benedikt Paul Göcke, and Ludwig Jaskolla, Innsbruck Studies in Philosophy of Religion 2 (Leiden and Boston, MA: Brill and Mentis, 2020), 205–30; Kallistos Ware, "God Immanent yet Transcendent: The Divine Energies According to Saint Gregory Palamas," in *In Whom We Live and Move and Have Our Being: Panentheistic Reflections on God's Presence in a Scientific World*, ed. Philip Clayton and Arthur Robert Peacocke (Grand Rapids, MI and Cambridge: Eerdmans, 2004), 157–68.

113 The expressions belong to John D. Barrow, *The Origin of the Universe*, Science Masters (New York: Basic Books, 1994), 45.

114 See Costache, "Maximus and John," 85, 87; "A Theology of the World," 210–12; "The Orthodox Doctrine of Creation," 48, 57, 58–60. See also Yannaras, *Elements of Faith*, 39–40. See also the contributions reunited in Martin A. Nowak and Sarah Coakley, eds., *Evolution, Games, and God: The Principle of Cooperation* (Cambridge, MA and London: Harvard University Press, 2013).

115 See Costache, *Humankind and the Cosmos*, chapters five and six.

116 Basil, *Homilies on the Hexaemeron* 2.3.

117 Basil, *Homilies on the Hexaemeron* 5.2 (see 8.1; 9.2).

118 Gregory of Nyssa, *An Apology for the Hexaemeron* 64; 65; 69. For Gregory's natural philosophy, see Katsos, *The Metaphysics of Light*, 76–91.

119 John Chrysostom, *Homilies on Genesis* 3.1.
120 See on this the comments of Costache, *Humankind and the Cosmos*, 251–54.
121 See Knight, *Eastern Orthodoxy*, 40–47.
122 See David Bradshaw, "The *Logoi* of Beings in Greek Patristic Thought," in *Toward an Ecology of Transfiguration*, 9–22; Costache, *Humankind and the Cosmos*, 61–108; Louth, *Introducing Eastern Orthodox Theology*, 41–43; Louth, "Man and Cosmos," 62–66.
123 Costache, *Humankind and the Cosmos*, 21, 234, 241, 244, 251, 255–57, 303–04.
124 Teilhard de Chardin, *Le phénomène humain*, 59, 60–62.
125 The phrase "cosmic revolutionaries" refers to the scientifically untrained deniers of contemporary cosmology. For what is expected of a new cosmological theory, see Luke A. Barnes and Geraint F. Lewis, *The Cosmic Revolutionary's Handbook (Or: How to Beat the Big Bang)* (Cambridge: Cambridge University Press, 2020), 9–20.
126 Knight, "Divine Action and the Laws of Nature," 49–51.
127 Clement, *Exhortation* 1.5.2.
128 Gregory the Theologian, *Discours (Orations)* 30.18.
129 Basil, *Homilies on the Hexaemeron* 9.2.
130 John Chrysostom, *Homilies on Genesis* 3.1.
131 Maximus, *The Mystagogy* 7; *Answers to Thalassius* 60.
132 Diadochus, *One Hundred Practical Texts* 75.13–16.
133 Gregory the Great, *Dialogues* 2.35.
134 Adomnán, *Life of Saint Columba* 1.1; 1.35. See Costache, *Humankind and the Cosmos*, n. 150 at 133–34, n. 218 at 320. This does not amount to the dissipation of the self in the great ocean of indistinct being advocated by Stellar, "Awe Helps Us Remember," 84.
135 Julian of Norwich, *A Vision Showed to a Devout Woman* 4.7–10. We are grateful to Carole Cusack for this reference.
136 Stăniloae, *Teologia dogmatică ortodoxă*, 3: 408, 420. See also Theokritoff, "Creator and creation," 69–70.
137 Lossky, *Mystical Theology*, 106.
138 See Frederick D. Aquino and Paul L. Gavrilyuk, eds., *Perceiving Things Divine: Towards a Constructive Account of Spiritual Perception* (Oxford: Oxford University Press, 2022); Paul L. Gavrilyuk and Sarah Coakley, eds., *The Spiritual Senses: Perceiving God in Western Christianity* (Cambridge: Cambridge University Press, 2012); Bronwen Neil, Doru Costache, and Kevin Wagner, *Dreams, Virtue and Divine Knowledge in Early Christian Egypt* (Cambridge: Cambridge University Press, 2019), 66–115.
139 See Acts 14:17.
140 As promised in Matthew 13:43. For these experiences, see Doru Costache, "Burning Hearts: Emmaus as Realised Eschatology in the *Philokalic* Tradition," in *God's Grace Inscribed on the Human Heart: Essays in Honour of James R. Harrison*, ed. Peter G. Bolt and Sehyun Kim, Early Christian Studies 23 (Macquarie Park: SCD Press, 2022), 61–78, esp. 66–71; Costache, *Humankind and the Cosmos*, 256–57; Doru Costache, "Adam's Holiness in the Alexandrine and Athonite Traditions,"

in *Alexandrian Legacy: A Critical Appraisal*, ed. Doru Costache, Philip Kariatlis, and Mario Baghos (Newcastle upon Tyne: Cambridge Scholars, 2015), 322–68, esp. 334–40.
141 Origen, *On First Principles* 2.3.6. See the explanation of John Behr, "Introduction," in *Origen: On First Principles*, 2 vols, ed. John Behr, Oxford Early Christian Texts (Oxford: Oxford University Press, 2017), 1: xv–xcviii, esp. liv.
142 See the recent monograph on levitating saints by agnostic author Carlos M. N. Eire, *They Flew: A History of the Impossible* (New Haven, CT: Yale University Press, 2023).
143 Teilhard de Chardin, *Le phénomène humain*, 52.
144 See John 2:11,23; 3:2; 4:54 etc.
145 See Romans 8:19–21.
146 See Revelation 21:1; 1 Corinthians 15:28; Ephesians 4:6.
147 See Maximus the Confessor, *Answers to Thalassius* 53.15; 63.518; 64.581.
148 See Costache, *Humankind and the Cosmos*, 52–58, 73–75, 120–31, 161–68, 201–06, 223–41, 292–97, 302–26; Costache, "Maximus and John," 87–91; Costache, "Mapping Reality," 380–81.

4 The Self and the Universe in the Age of Science

For Another Copernican Turn

One of the most challenging topics for cosmology and theology alike is the function and destiny of the self, or consciousness, in the universe. It is to this unknown that we now turn. We discuss the impact of modern and contemporary cosmological ideas upon the self itself, on an existential level, and upon representations of the self's role in the world. First, we focus on the self's alienation triggered by the realisation of the infinite universe—beyond the Copernican Turn and the modern return to the ancient heliocentric paradigm.[1] Second, we suggest ways of restoring the self's sense of worth and retrieving meaning, including by doing cosmology and contemplating the natural world. At least as known to the Orthodox tradition, nature contemplation is a comprehensive framework for connecting the self and the universe, the subject and the object, as it were, at the crossing of various disciplinary perspectives, ways of knowing, and levels of perception.

We hope to show that the Orthodox tradition has the potential to become a significant contributor to the conversation about the destiny of the self in the universe, which marks what promises to become a New Copernican Turn in contemporary culture. As anticipated in our brief discussion about panpsychism and panentheism in Chapter Three, a cultural shift towards drawing the self and the cosmos together is at hand, though not a return to human interiority at the expense of the world. This final part takes up the story from where the end of Chapter Two and the beginning of Chapter Three left it and engages further sources in order to sketch a broader picture of the topic. Whether cosmologists would find this proposal interesting is doubtful, at least when it comes to their profession, but they, like many other contemporaries, might catch a glimpse of something else here pertaining to the existential side of things.

The Predicament of the Self

One of the nine subtitles of Walker Percy's book captures the topic of the self and the universe with utmost clarity, also dramatically, as well as with irony: "How you can survive in the Cosmos about which you know more and

DOI: 10.4324/9781003527138-4

more while knowing less and less about yourself."[2] This subtitle alludes to contemporary cosmology and its impact on our consciousness, rather our perception of the self in the world. We push forward, Percy says, expanding our knowledge of the universe, and in the process, we—Pascal's "thinking reeds"[3]—lose sight of ourselves. But Percy's sentence can likewise refer to fields of study. If so, it indicates the disproportionate development of the natural sciences compared to the humanities. While the former thrive, the latter distance themselves from their spirit, scope, and aims by lamely applying quantitative measures to human experiences.[4] In both cases, that is, existential and disciplinary, to make sense of the human person, the self, Percy tells us, is destined to fail.

In the wake of the Copernican Turn—including its recent instantiations, the decentralised infinite universe and the multiverse, with their plethora of cultural reverberations—real people and their experiences have become an uninteresting object of study and a misunderstood one, at that, leading to the self's ignorance of itself. Kurt Vonnegut formulated a similar idea when he wrote, "Mankind, ignorant of the truths that lie within every human being, looked outward—pushed ever outward."[5] The consensus is evident, and we would not discount the possibility of Percy having found inspiration in Vonnegut's thought.

The same subtitle of Percy's book mentions the self's struggle for survival, denoting the existential crisis most people currently experience. People see themselves as condemned to live in a universe perceived as irrelevant and void of meaning, the universe of *sola scriptura* and related ideas, where no hope is possible. In Vonnegut's words, "a nightmare of meaninglessness without end."[6] And people do not fare well. They admire the beauty of cosmic landscapes through the eyes of powerful telescopes but find no comfort in the universe's depressing pointlessness, as well as in thinking, for that matter. Pascal's reference to people as thinking reeds does not inspire them with pride and confidence any longer. No wonder a terror deeper than Steven Weinberg's take on our futility undermines people's emotional balance and wellbeing. In Weinberg's words,

> The more the universe seems comprehensible, the more it also seems pointless . . . The effort to understand the universe is one of the very few things that lifts human life a little above the level of farce, and gives it some of the grace of tragedy.[7]

Mind the absence of the self from this statement. Percy, too, refers to "the comic mystery of . . . existence,"[8] with Vonnegut, earlier, characterising the human adventure in the age of science and technology as "empty heroics, low comedy, and pointless death."[9] Teilhard, earlier still, believed that modern science has transformed people into "erratic objects in a disjointed World."[10] The thinking reeds are downgraded to reeds—subjects to objects.

Weinberg sums up the worst news contemporary cosmology brings, that is, when it comes to our quest for order, beauty, meaning, and purpose in the universe, all boils down to nothing. Or, at best, to ones and zeroes. This perception is not new. Here, Weinberg echoes Pascal's rhetorical claims referred to in Chapter Three about the frightening silence of a universe whose vastness overwhelms human comprehension.[11] We say "rhetorical" because Pascal did not cower before this troubling perspective, as we shall soon discover. Regardless, the news isn't good for the self. As Sabine Hossenfelder notes, contemporary cosmology effects a "shift in how we perceive our own relevance in the world (or lack thereof)."[12]

The perspective of infinite space and the "tasteless, weightless sea of outwardness without end," in Vonnegut's words,[13] is repellent to the human mind, the self. "The simple truth is that interstellar distances will not fit into the human imagination," Douglas Adams adds.[14] Our experience does not include large cosmic scales. When we look up, what we see is the roof of a home, as we did for a million years, not an endless, silent immensity. We are earthbound, environmentally conditioned beings.[15] No wonder the infinite universe is of no concern to most people. Nevertheless, it causes distress to those who ponder it from an existential angle, especially if no hope spurs their *joie de vivre*. The latter group seems to react in two different ways to the horror of the boundless cosmos. Percy describes these reactions as "transcendence" through science and art, by which the person affirms itself arrogantly, in splendid abstraction from reality, and "immanence," usually associated with consumerism, typical for a resigned attitude.[16] Nothing ultimately helps. Neither arrogant transcendence nor resigned immanence can fill the void within. Not even asserting the self over and against nature through violent exploitation could restore its significance in a world whose contours fade into the inscrutable horizons of infinity.

In response to the impressive extent of our knowledge about almost nothing—the five per cent of the known universe, as discussed in the second chapter of this book, with the downside of the self's reduction to an organism wholly dependent on its artificial environment[17]—in their desperate attempt to be, to assert themselves, people lose their bearing. Percy's analysis is merciless at this juncture. People experience disappointment after disappointment with science itself—including the "debilitating strictures of modern psychology, which has not the means of saying anything at all about the self, let alone spirit"[18]—and with work, family, school, politics, church, and social life.[19]

The ultimate terror, however, is not the fact of being "lost in the cosmos"—in Weinberg's meaninglessness of the spacetime continuum or in Vonnegut's outwardness without end, deprived as we are of internal geodesics in the chaos of knowing and unknowing. For, as Percy says, people are no longer "inner-directed"; they are "other-directed."[20] It is not merely that. In another subtitle of his book, Percy returns to this topic and brings to the fore, as ironical and indirect as ever, a new aspect of the situation: "Why it is that of all the billions and billions of strange objects in the Cosmos—novas, quasars, pulsars, black holes—you are beyond doubt the strangest."[21] Humanity's final terror is not the fact of being lost in space, figuratively or literally, within a silent universe whose vastness dwarves the self to insignificance; it is the fact of having no grasp of itself, thinking reeds though people might still be.

The source of this ultimate terror is the fact of the self ignoring itself; knowing and unknowing the universe comes second. It is not cosmology, therefore, that shatters people's dreams and reduces their lives to a farce. Nor is *sola scriptura*, with its *tabula rasa* universe, for that matter. It is the self's own strangeness that eludes our grasp. For the self evades all computation and quantitative measurements, the mathematical apparatus needed to know the outer world. And, unfortunately, our scientific and technological culture has forgotten about other ways of measuring things like the self. Even the humanities have stopped being humane.[22] No wonder the self ignores itself. Percy aptly notes that "we don't seem to know much more about the psyche than Plato did."[23]

This is a very optimistic appraisal of the situation since Plato, his classical successors, and his early Christian progeny knew the self better than we do. They were fascinated with the "soul" and with introspection and other ways of knowing the self.[24] This fascination led some of them, such as Evagrius, to the point of discussing the self under the guise of sophisticated cosmological systems.[25] This consuming interest was a preemptive strike at the growing body of knowledge about the outer, physical rims of reality, a crusade in the name of the self or a metaphysics of the self. These ancients faced a crisis that anticipated our own, but chose to solve it by consolidating the self's grasp of itself, not through resignation. This led to a mature psychology, or science of the self, as Percy himself suggests in the previous remark, long before modern psychology. The modern sense that the self eludes its own grasp is integral to the issue at hand, namely, the fact of ignoring where the self is at in relation to understanding itself in this age of science and within a universe whose boundaries have been pushed far beyond our line of sight. The major difference between the modern crisis of the self and Plato's concerns is that we do not seem able to find a way out—although Nesteruk's own turn from cosmology to anthropology, mentioned in the introduction to this book, might yield some results to that end.

Before we look for solutions, however, we must ask ourselves what could be so problematic about contemporary cosmology itself, with its mathematical models and its overwhelmingly vast universe, theorised as but a bubble in the endless matrix of the multiverse. The answer, as we have seen at the end of Chapter Two, is simple: cosmology excludes the self from its calculations, while the subjects, or the selves, refuse to be taken out of the equation. In Pascal's words,

> Human beings are but reeds, the weakest beings in nature, but thinking reeds nonetheless. You won't need the whole of the universe to crush

them; a wisp of gas or a drop of water would suffice to kill them. But though the universe could easily crush human beings, they would still be nobler compared to what kills them—for they will know both that they die and the advantage the universe has on them. The universe, in turn, knows nothing.[26]

It is at this juncture that we understand the deep meaning of Pascal's cry upon realising the universe's silent vastness. This desperate cry was not the expression of his own angst; it was the voice of the anonymous many who were unable to articulate their terror. In turn, Pascal knew that what defines the self are its mind, thoughts, experiences, desires, and emotions, not quantitative measurements. The same goes for Augustine, as we saw earlier in this book, as well as for Pascal's colleague, Descartes. Is this not the reason why Descartes had discerned the "thinking thing" and the "spaced thing," the self and the cosmos?[27] Similarly, and echoing the Platonic tradition, Christian and otherwise, Pascal concludes:

> It is not in space at all that I must seek my dignity; it is in organising my thinking. I would gain nothing by possessing lands. True, the universe apprehends and swallows me within its space as though I were a meagre dot. Still, by my thinking I understand it.[28]

Weinberg's terrible news draws upon this conclusion, but an important difference remains. Pascal considers thinking and knowing an Archimedean point for asserting humanity, for making a dent in the fabric of reality.[29] In turn, Weinberg takes thinking and knowing as the only things available to us when all else becomes impossible and futile. He looks at the empty half of the cup.

As we know, however, in the long run, thinking and knowing could not lift us up by much above "the level of farce," to paraphrase Weinberg again, especially when thinking and knowing no longer include the self—as happens in the natural sciences by default, in the alienated humanities that embrace objectivism and quantitative criteria, and in cold political and economic calculations. This renders many people unhappy, agnostic and religious alike. Nevertheless, the self cannot be reduced to thinking and knowing anyway. Humankind's interactions with its immediate environment and the wider setting of the universe are more complex than any intellectual grasp of things. And while our culture is shaken from time to time by the realisation of some of us, like William Shatner, of the smallness and fragility of the Earth against the cosmic background,[30] Mircea Eliade had shown that both *homo religiosus* and its secular descendants thirst to participate in the plenitude of reality.[31] The self is inherent to the cosmos. Accordingly, Athanasius acknowledges humanity as a "part of the universe as much as the rest" of it.[32] His point denotes a complex view of the human and the cosmic, a modern expression of which is Percy's ternary idea of reality. Corresponding to Karl Popper's "third world" situated at the intersection of subject and object[33] and Nicolescu's "ternary dialectic of reality" that does not lend itself to reductionist thinking,[34] Percy's reality has tridimensional consistency. It includes the social interaction of the selves that live in the world and exchange messages about it.[35] This socially, culturally, and symbolically constructed universe—an objective reality experienced subjectively—differs from the binary scientific discourse that ignores the selves, with their aspirations and desires.[36] In Adam Frank's simple words, "for us, reality is experience."[37]

Not so in many places, especially in the natural sciences, which causes distress. Conditioned by the "anomaly of objectivism," Percy notes, "scientists don't have to take account of themselves and other selves in their science."[38] They substitute the self's perception of the cosmos—and the exchange of news about it between the selves—with equations and strings of ones and zeroes. As Frank characterises it, modern physics "is a perfectly objective perspective on a perfectly objective reality existing without reference to life or human experience."[39] And while, quantitatively, the strings of ones and zeroes might sometimes point to something real, qualitatively or existentially, they are meaningless. The ones and the zeroes bypass people and their meaningful communication among themselves. And so, concludes Percy, "the science of the scientist can understand everything in the Cosmos but the self of the scientist."[40] This conclusion captures with utmost clarity the predicament of the self, which finds no room for itself either in the universe or in the natural sciences as models of reality.[41] This is a serious issue. Tom McLeish showed how corrosive for the self the departure of modern culture from the world and from science understood as *shared* experiences proved to be.[42] The opposite of the tridimensional world of complex relations is existential impoverishment.

The exclusion of the self and its fellow selves from the natural sciences, as well as from other places, opposes everything we humans stand for; in a sense, it is inhuman. The sciences are our creation, but their scope and aims do not include us any longer. Ignoring any existential centre, they paint the surrealistic image of a meaningless reality that renders the self an exile. Teilhard was right to warn us about the tendency of the natural sciences to relegate consciousness, the self, to the menagerie of curiosities,[43] the irrelevancies of the universe. The situation is unbearable. And it is more so because the modern self—separated from Platonic wisdom—balked when the sciences excluded it from the algorithms of reality. Percy comments dryly, "difficulties arise when triadic creatures (scientists) try to explain evolution [and other scientific facts] through exclusively dyadic events" that reduce reality to objects and to objectivist hypotheses about them.[44]

The self enjoys tridimensionality or, as Margaret Somerville has it, spirituality, understood as "a deeply intuitive sense of relatedness or connectedness to all life, especially other people, to the world, and to the universe in which we live," as well as a "longing for transcendence—the strong desire to experience the feeling of belonging to something larger than ourselves."[45] In Nicolescu's words, inherent to the self is a "transreligious attitude"

> which links beings and things and . . . induces in the very depths of the human being an absolute respect for others, to whom he or she is linked by their sharing a common life on one and the same Earth.[46]

In short, the self is that being that, in Percy's words, "has an environment, but it also has a world."[47] Its complex world results from the selves' sociocultural transactions of giving and receiving signs about everything, even nature itself.

On the other side of the iron curtain, Stăniloae made the same point in 1979, namely, that the world is not only an object; it is the content of what people tell each other about it, a shared reality.[48] Likewise, Orthodox philosopher Bruce Foltz calls this shared dimension of the world "iconic," that is, endowed with relational, contextual, epiphanic, and personal dimensions.[49] In the absence of the world as a socially shared reality—as a sign given and received—the self has no place to lay its head, to paraphrase a known trope, and everything turns existentially meaningless, causing the crisis we now face. This is where the natural sciences, certain quarters of the humanities, and especially cosmology become abhorrent. The widespread resistance of contemporary cosmologists to the anthropic principle—with its commonsense link between the human phenomenon, the fact that we are here, and the universe[50]—says it all. It comes easier to them to contemplate the hideaways of dark energy or the cosmic web of galaxies or the multiverse's nirvana, the total bliss of the self's annihilation. This is a twisted Cartesian kind of thinking, for Descartes, like Pascal, Plato, and their entire philosophical lineage, wished to secure the qualitative nature of the self's experiences, not to facilitate its quantitative elimination from among the things that matter. As Percy describes the situation,

> Every advance in an objective understanding of the Cosmos and in its technological control further distances the self from the Cosmos precisely in the degree of the advance—so that in the end the self becomes a space-bound ghost which roams the very Cosmos it understands perfectly.[51]

Very well said. As the quantitative assessments at work in science and technology remain wholly inapplicable to itself, the self that birthed science and technology finds itself unwillingly exiled from its own discoveries and inventions, not only from the boundless universe the sciences reveal. It is here, however, from this nadir of the self's crisis that its ascent becomes possible.

The Return of the Self

There is an element of exaggeration to Percy's previous statement, an assumption that usually goes unchallenged. It is the conviction that we understand the universe perfectly. No wonder we feel so uneasy about the self, which remains, as we have seen previously, a mystery to us, an unknown.

As mystical concepts such as dark matter and dark energy have become widespread, we can be more realistic than this. Chapter Two shows that we do not know more than five per cent of the universe, with this figure seemingly representing an optimistic assessment of the situation. Adams expresses these proportions with clarity: as "time blossomed" together with the expansion of the universe, "matter shrank away."[52] The same goes for our grasp of things. It would be closer to the truth to say that we know immensely about a mere fraction of reality, that we train our minds and instruments upon whatever our science and technology make available to us while we ignore what our mathematics does not dream of and tools cannot reach. In short, physics and cosmology are as blind to the dark side of reality as they are to the supernatural and to the self itself. The best they can do about the hidden parts of reality—Teilhard's *dedans*[53]—is acknowledge their existence, which they generously grant when it comes to dark matter and dark energy. We therefore concur with H. P. Lovecraft's assessment that "though the area of the unknown has been steadily contracting for thousands of years, an infinite reservoir of mystery still engulfs most of the outer cosmos."[54] But, as they come near Plank's Wall, so to speak, in regard to the dark side of reality, will the natural sciences factor in the existence and the role of the self? We do hope so, for the sake of science and for the thinking reeds that we are.

The shrinking self should stop feeling lost and hopeless. The universe is unimaginably vast and strange, indeed, but the sciences are far from being able to exhaust its mystery. The self is not the only unknown. Our mathematics can grasp neither the universe nor the self nor more exotic dwellers of the jungle of numbers nor many other things in the world for, as Penrose shows, reality resists computation.[55] In his words, "the world might . . . be deterministic but *non-computable*." While causality is at work, it is difficult, if not altogether impossible, to model or to represent it mathematically—including, for example, how the present state of things determines the future. The "dark side" fits this profile to a tee. Furthermore, Penrose continues, this could have an impact on what we think about the self and its salient properties. Thus, "the free will that we believe ourselves to be capable of would have to be intimately tied in with some *non-computable* ingredient in the laws that govern the world in which we actually live."[56] The self and the universe are of one piece, the two sides of one coin. And, Penrose adds, this "*non-computable* ingredient" built within the natural laws, in turn, could elude us forever.[57] The self is as mysterious as the universe is. Penrose gives hope to the exiled self by showing it that reality, overall, is as strange as it, the self, is. This might not be the best news the self would expect to receive. There are ways that are definitely more successful than others when it comes to rescuing it from its modern predicament. But what matters is that solutions are foreseeable and that the self should stop feeling despondent in the universe as contemporary cosmology describes it.

We have seen that, for Percy, doing science and cultivating the arts are attempts at transcending the self's sense of not belonging. But are doing science and cultivating the arts affordable solutions for all? Could all of us, or at least many of us, be scientists or artists? Obviously not. However, before we move on to seek an alternative way of retrieving the self, we should remember that thinking, researching, and knowing do not suffice. How could they, when we know so little about the universe we thought we knew so well? How could they, when scientists themselves appear to be "lost in math," as Hossenfelder has it, and seem to understand physics less and less?[58] And how could they, since "logic alone will not suffice to find the right theory," when "there are many things that are mathematically consistent that have nothing to do with the world"?[59] The same goes for other areas of scientific enquiry, including the psychological exploration of the self, each new discovery raising new questions and opening up more abysses of mystery before us. And the same holds true for the arts, which, Percy notes, are equally unable to lift the spirits of the depressed self.[60]

We have already hit Planck's Wall, epistemologically and aesthetically speaking, without being able to crack it; attempting to transcend our insignificance through science and the arts cannot help us much. Does this mean, then, that we should abandon the quest and get drowned in consumerism or other forms of resignation? Not at all. Humankind's wisdom traditions point to alternate routes, roads less taken by the modern self, the arts, the sciences, and the technology it has generated. One such route could be the ancient Minoan worldview that, according to Jack Dempsey, artfully sketches "a cosmos that both nurtures and ignores the individual"[61]—one that makes the self feel at home without losing sight of its context, without switching back to the selfish, anthropocentric default. Another avenue could be the prehistoric integration of life, craft, and worldview (as revealed by archaeoastronomy; see Figure 4.1), whose patterns reverberate through the ages, being foundational for the experience of traditional societies that survive to this day.[62] But in what follows, we shall focus on an example immediately relevant here.

Orthodox Christianity gives an indirect response to the self's undertaking to escape its predicament by welcoming the problem rather than circumventing it. The advice for the marginalised and the exiled is to embrace marginalisation and exile. "Have the mentality of an exile in the place where you live," says Abba Poemen, a desert elder.[63] The self should not ignore its own angst and misery. To render this lesson relevant to the topic under consideration, adapting Pascal's stance, the self should acknowledge its own quantitative insignificance within the infinite universe and the fact of being dispossessed

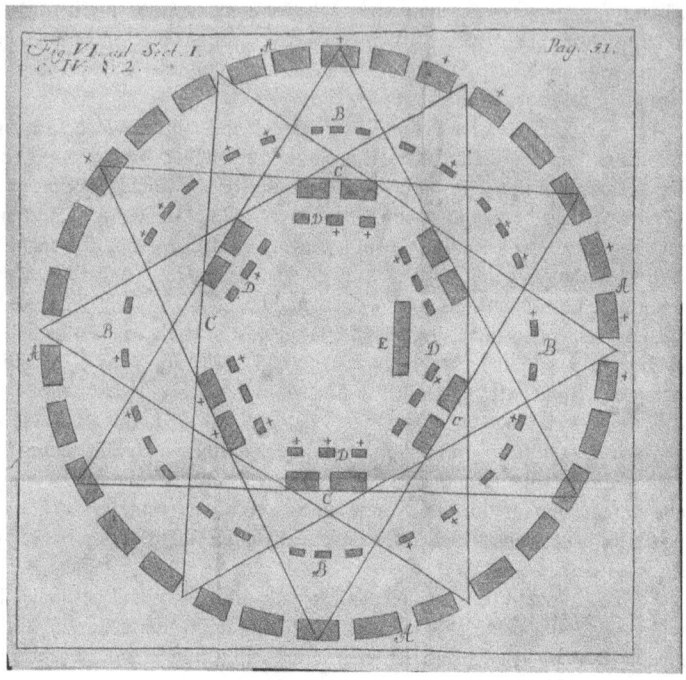

Figure 4.1 A Model of Stonehenge. The image shows item 6 at page 51 of Johann Georg Keyssler's book, *Antiquitates selectae septentrionales et Celticae* (Hanover, 1790). It presents a schematic depiction of Stonehenge as an example of prehistoric symbolic cosmos, where astronomical and life rhythms are culturally immortalised.[64]

of its symbolic world by *sola scriptura* and the rationalisations of modern science. It should relish, as Donald Rumsfeld would have it, the knowns and the unknowns, the known knowns and the known unknowns, the unknown knowns and the unknown unknowns of its condition.[65] This would correspond to adopting a humble mindset conducive to a realistic appraisal of life. Then, it should do something about this situation to earn its own significance in the world. Romanian philosopher and poet Lucian Blaga welcomed the "mystery's horizon" as a way of grasping reality and the self's place amidst all things,[66] "articulating the metaphysical mystery as mystery" instead of seeking to bypass it.[67] The articulation of mysteries as such and the analytical "transfiguration of antinomies" by the operations of the "ecstatic intellect" dubbed "minus-knowledge" intensify the mystery of existence.[68] This led to a deep appreciation of mysteries found everywhere, far and near, and to the self's enjoyment in the world. Accordingly, the poet sang:

> I do not crush the world's corolla of wonders
> and do not kill
> with my mind the mysteries I encounter
> on my way.[69]

In the third chapter of this book, we referred to this approach as apophaticism, understood as a humble acceptance of our limitations when it comes to knowing things. This form of intellectual exile, apophaticism, is willing, not unwilling; it is not defeat. It does not sacrifice either the cosmos for the sake of the self seen as the only reality or the self for the purposes of making the cosmos intelligible by ones and zeroes. As such, it promises brighter perspectives for the self in the world and for our understanding of the universe. As with Somerville's "Wonder Equation," it promises more than comprehensiveness and responsibility; it promises joy.[70] Here is the equation: $AWA + (S - (C + N)) => G + H => E$. In verbal transcription, it goes as follows:

> "Amazement wonder and awe" (AWA) plus (healthy) skepticism(S), that is minus cynicism(C) and minus nihilism(N), can elicit deep gratitude(G), including for life, and hope(H) the oxygen of the human spirit, which, in turn, can lead to ethics(E)—a concern to act ethically—and, I would tentatively add, to joy.[71]

We shall soon discover that this outcome is what other thinkers have been seeking.

However, while the apophatic approach is an important step towards retrieving the self in the world, it by no means exhausts the process. Percy advises the self directly, "like Copernicus and Einstein, turn the universe upside down and begin with a new assumption."[72] The self should initiate another Copernican Turn by thinking otherwise. Pascal seems to anticipate this step when he sets as our task to "work on thinking well."[73] But will the self be able to agree to its exile in order to transform it into the roadmap of its own return? How will it execute the New Copernican Turn, this time round, from being "other-directed" to being "inner-directed"?[74] And will the self be able to do so without losing sight of the outer world, of the starry sky and all its wonders—without abandoning the dream of travelling *ad astra*? For the point is not in fulfilling Vonnegut's prophecy that "outwardness lost, at last, its imagined attractions. Only inwardness remained to be explored. Only the human soul remained *terra incognita*."[75] Nor is it about adhering to Pascal's related proposal, to ignore the vastness of the cosmos—space and duration—and to focus entirely on the self's capacity for ratiocination.[76]

The challenge of the New Copernican Turn is to bridge Descartes' two worlds, the "thinking thing" and the "spaced thing," Teilhard's *dedans* and *dehors*, Bohm's "thought and non-thought," "the thing and the thought," or "the physical and mental sides of reality,"[77] or again, in Nesteruk's terms, "cosmology and anthropology as two parts of the book of being."[78] In Teilhard's footsteps,[79] but somehow echoing Percy's point about thinking otherwise, Nesteruk does just that, along the lines of the anthropic cosmological principle. As he notes: "Humanity is not inserted in the allegedly preexisting cosmic history but, on the contrary, cosmological evolution has its origin in the history of the human as that primary and inherent existential beginning of any possible articulation of the world."[80]

This is a bold thought which defies conventional thinking. Thinking well, in this case, is to realise that the story should be read from the other end, of the subject, not of the object; of the self, not of the cosmos. Nesteruk's idea is not new to the Orthodox tradition and its ancient sources. Another challenging thought was put forward by Gregory the Theologian, who referred counterintuitively to the human being as macrocosm, or great world, located in the universe as microcosm, or small world.[81] What caused this metaphorical reversal is the understanding of the human being as the hub where all of reality, visible and invisible, intersects and reaches a higher level of organisation. Maximus the Confessor developed his thought by describing the human being as encompassing the cosmos and as encoding the final shape of the universe.[82] In terms of our age, this reversal would suggest that, qualitatively, the human being is more complex than the universe and that it is through this complex model that we should consider the whole. This view of things heralds a revolutionary understanding of the relationship between the self and the cosmos, without which the return of the self appears to be impossible. And while believers find poetic signposts of this revolution in the eighth Psalm (verses 3–8), in Gregory the Theologian's model, in the bold statement of Nesteruk, quoted previously, and in Louth's reinterpretation of Maximus in conversation with Pascal,[83] the secular self will need a different kind of map.

Several stages can be foreseen, paving the way for the self's return. First, the exiled self will have to learn mathematics in order to speak the language of the country of exile, the land of physics and cosmology. This is what Pythagoras and Plato did in order to make possible the self's return in antiquity. Their solution is still appealing, after a fashion, given the mathematical infrastructure of reality. Carl Sagan set in pages of fictional prose the possibility that "in the fabric of space and in the nature of matter, as in a great work of art, there is, written small, the artist's signature."[84] His artist is not God. What he means is a universe-making intelligence, a race of advanced selves who left a hidden mathematical footprint in the matrix of reality. Deciphering this signature, or message, its mathematical language, is the most important task of the self. Neither the fictional context of this discussion nor the extraterrestrial reference is of consequence here. What matters is the point about the self rising above insignificance by learning the language of its exile, by not giving up. It could achieve the same outcome, alternatively, to paraphrase Somerville, by "living comfortably with uncertainty in order to gain insight."[85]

Second, the self will have to find enjoyment in crunching numbers, measuring things, weighing stuff, and theorising about all things in heaven and on earth, knowns and unknowns alike. This is, as Roger Wagner and Andrew Briggs noted, the path taken by Clement of Alexandria, who pursued knowledge and research without abandoning theological thinking.[86] And this is what Abraham did in Clement's rewriting of the story.[87] Third, the self should learn that there are people out there—many scientists among them, not only the panpsychists earlier mentioned—who identify either the self or something like it as the foundation of things, calling it, as, for instance, John Barrow does, an "underlying rationality" that transcends the material universe.[88] In like manner, Paul Davies observes the following:

> Far from exposing human beings as incidental products of blind physical forces, science suggests that the existence of conscious organisms is a *fundamental* feature of the universe. We have been written into the laws of nature in a deep and, I believe, meaningful way.[89]

Again, this is not a new thought. When Gregory of Nyssa pointed out that "everything that comes into being is generated by reason"[90] and that *soul* is the content of various layers of reality,[91] he echoed an already venerable philosophical tradition whose roots go deep, to prehistoric spirituality.[92] The same wisdom inspired Teilhard, mentioned throughout this book, and the fact that contemporary scientists express related views is encouraging. The self should keep an eye on where the ideas of Bohm, Roger Penrose, Henry Stapp, and others like them[93] will lead our culture next. It, the self, might soon learn that its exile is epistemological, so to speak, not ontological, and that the universe is not as meaningless and mute as it thought it is.

Fourth, the self will have to connect the dots to bridge the inner and the outer worlds, Teilhard's *dedans* and *dehors*, perhaps by way of semiotics. At least, this is what La Matina considers to be the challenge of our times. He militates for the transformation of contemporary sciences by linking the objects and the subjects of knowledge via transitional fields and the liminality of distal zones, whose infrastructural nexus the scientific method currently ignores.[94] At the centre of his solution is the person, the self, connected with the whole of reality.[95] Percy, a semiotician himself, would have greatly rejoiced at learning about this avenue of thought. This and similar proposals entail to interiorise science, reclaim its humanity, and bring it back into the service of the self and its flourishing in the world. We shall say a few more things about this a little later when summarising McLeish's views. Already, Arthur Koestler signalled the urgency of banding together the mystic and the scientist.[96] To that end, contemplation appears to be quite useful, Foltz agrees,[97] without being the only way for the self to execute the New Copernican Turn, its own return. With this matter we shall concern ourselves in the remaining part of this chapter.

The Contemplative Self, Past and Present

The self might feel disappointed by Nikos Kazantzakis' following point: "since we cannot change reality, let us change the eyes which see reality."[98] The enthusiastic self is always eager to assert itself, and changing the world seems the best way to do so. Hence, its disappointment at the prospect of not succeeding. This feeling matches the sorrow of Barnes and Lewis' "cosmic revolutionaries" when their untestable ideas are rejected. But Kazantzakis does not mean to discourage the self. He points to a better, historically tested way of affirming the self through its thoughtful connection with the world. What he refers to is the contemplation of nature, the topic of this final part of the chapter, and more—for to see, at least in the sense of his "Cretan Glance,"[99] is to change things truly and be changed in the process. Kazantzakis conveys the same message in his novel about Francis of Assisi, where he proposes a crescendo from seeing to interpreting to transforming nature.

First, his Francis opens the eyes and sees the world with its charming beauty:

> Each dawn, when the birds begin to sing again, or at midday when he plunged into the cooling shade of the forest, or at night, sitting in the moonlight or beneath the stars, he would shudder from inexpressible joy and gaze at me, his eyes filled with tears. "What miracles these are, Brother Leo!" he would say. "And He who created such beauty—what then must He be? What can we call Him?"[100]

No ones and zeroes in this way of considering reality. No sense of being lost in the silent vastness of the universe. From the observer's familiar surroundings to the remotest visible rim of reality, there is no vacuum. Beings, beautiful beings, both animate and inanimate, fill all conceivable niches. It should not come as a surprise that the self experiences pure joy at the vast complexity of the world of which it is a part, while the thought of the believer moves to and fro between enjoying cosmic beauty and wondering about the creator.[101] Awareness of beauty leaves no room for the terror of a mute, meaningless universe. And what Kazantzakis' Francis discovers through the beauty of nature is not an "interventionist god," disruptive supernatural agencies, in the Western sense of the idea. Reminiscent of Paul's Areopagus speech,[102] he finds out the warm, loving, fertile womb of reality. Accordingly, Francis responds, "No, not God, not God . . . That name is heavy, it crushes bones . . . Not God—Father!"[103] Nature, with its beauty, is not terrible; it is inviting and welcoming, finely tuned for life, and so, too, is nature's maker, a welcoming presence. This realisation leads Francis to the next stage of the contemplative process, of interpreting nature theologically. This new stage reveals the link and the familiarity of the created and the uncreated, where one reveals itself under the guise of the other:

> "Beauty is God's daughter," said Francis as he gazed out through the open window at the yard, the vine arbor, the scattered white clouds that were cruising in the sky. "Beauty is God's daughter: that I'm sure of. The only way we can divine the appearance of God's face is by looking at beautiful things."[104]

The complex beauty of the cosmos is meaningful, revealing the creator's character by way of the creation's fitness and charm. The impact of a long and lasting wisdom tradition transpires here.[105] But things do not end with this theologically meaningful perception of the world. This perception engenders a sense of responsibility for the destiny of the world. Once it is theologically edified through reflecting upon cosmic beauty, the insightful self begins to work in God's own manner. Kazantzakis summarises Francis' wisdom as follows:

> For me Saint Francis is the model of the dutiful man, the man who by means of ceaseless ... struggle succeeds in fulfilling our highest obligation, something higher even than morality or truth or beauty: the obligation to transubstantiate the matter which God entrusted to us, and turn it into spirit.[106]

This point reminds us of Lossky and Stăniloae's vision of the eschatologically spiritualised world, discussed towards the end of Chapter Three. Undoubtedly, Kazantzakis tapped into the same sources of patristic wisdom that shaped the thinking of his two contemporaries. But, here, he meant more than the usual idea of the divine blueprint of a creation that moves towards future glory, hinting at the deliberate commitment of the contemplative self to the task of fulfilling the divine plan. To see things differently entails the self's transformation and is the way of transforming it. This, too, is a known patristic trope with modern Orthodox reverberations.[107]

One might wonder what prompted us to introduce this last part of our discourse on the New Copernican Turn by reviewing the ideas of authors who do not illustrate mainstream Orthodox Christian thinking. We did so knowing that, unfortunately, it is rather among exiles such as Blaga and Kazantzakis that the traditional Orthodox worldview can often be found, whereas mainstream thinkers ignore both nature and the natural sciences as a result of growing oblivious of their own tradition. This is problematic. By showing little or no interest in nature and in the sciences that study it, the frightened self, believing or otherwise, cannot heal itself. We have learnt that the self must embrace its exile in order to find itself a home.

Kazantzakis' direct contemplation of nature is just one way of returning home, but one replete with traditional overtones. Nevertheless, as we shall discover in what follows, the richness of the patristic tradition exceeds his proposal, sometimes bringing to bear the mediation of the available sciences in addition to the self's direct gaze upon the universe.

Patristic Ways of Contemplation

We now turn to nature contemplation as a way of vindicating the self while helping it to land in the thick and thin of things—to stop being an aimless wanderer in the world, as Tolkien would have it.[108] We begin by reviewing the contributions of two early Alexandrian thinkers, Clement and Athanasius, whose structured approaches Kazantzakis' own echoed, regardless of whether a direct influence can be established or not. As shown just previously, these methods incorporate information from the available sciences, or natural philosophies, as the ancients called them.

Athanasius sketches two approaches to nature contemplation, one focusing upon the self, or the "mindful soul,"[109] and the other on the cosmos.[110] These approaches are integral to a broader epistemology, whose details are of no concern here.[111] The first approach includes introspection, soul travel, and divine vision, referred to in terms that are reminiscent of the Platonic tradition[112] but accompanied by salient Christian elements such as faith, grace, and ascesis.[113] And while one might entertain the hope, with Vonnegut, that "everyone now knows how to find the meaning of life within himself,"[114] or comprehend reality, for that matter, Athanasius holds the contrary view. He shows that the "mindful soul" can attain true knowledge of itself, the universe, and God only when it undergoes gracious enhancement, theological guidance, and ascetic purification. These boost its intellective capabilities beyond what counts as their normal way of functioning.[115] Equipped with what Athanasius calls "divine sense perception,"[116] the self's grasp of reality exceeds what other ancient ways of knowing made possible.[117] The same goes for modern ways of knowing, which, as far as we can tell, have not yet reached the perception of the universe as a "single ray of the sun,"[118] earlier discussed, an unusual grasp of things to which Athanasius and his traditional peers alluded time and again.

This atypical perception corresponds to the permeating gaze mentioned in *Popol Vuh* (to add a broader religious perspective), of paradisal people able to see through solid objects,[119] to the self's perception of itself "in its proper state, which looks like a sapphire" in Evagrius Ponticus,[120] and to Pseudo-Macarius' contemplation of the self as the throne of divine glory.[121] Neither case allows for a natural insight without the self's spiritual transformation. What matters is that, within this unusual context, introspection leads to a profound knowledge of the self within itself and against the backdrop of a complex reality, at once natural and supernatural.

The second Athanasian approach includes curiosity about and research into the nature and harmony of the world. Echoing the unusual enhancements discussed above, Athanasius' paradisal Adam—resembling a "Platonic mystic," as Eginhard Meijering has it[122]—surveyed reality with pure eyes, full of wonder and insight, perceiving the creator and the creation together.[123] And while this level of perception remains the province of saints like Athanasius' hero, Antony,[124] intellectual tools and curricular training are nevertheless welcomed. The point about "contemplating and researching the beings,"[125] where "research" translates ἐπιστήμη, "science," captures both approaches. This amounts to an interdisciplinary quest for knowledge, which can be undertaken from either of the two ends.

Athanasius envisaged several stages of this quest, but he did not bother to set them in any order. One objective of research is to realise the "weakness, fluidity, and mortality" of the cosmos,[126] as mentioned in Chapter Three. Attentive research then leads to a sense of the unity of all distinct beings[127] whose foretaste is the realisation of humanity's belonging with the rest of the universe, discussed earlier. Then, guided by faith convictions, the contemplative self proceeds to identify signs of divine providence. A string of analogies helps articulate the findings. For example, as the lyre's music points to the skills of the musician who plays the song, the ordered universe denotes its maker's wisdom and caretaking.[128] Next, the contemplative self advances to higher gnosis and perceives the creation from a divine vantage point, that is, divinely. This leads to a perception of the world as God's creation and as an object of divine love.[129] This exercise is conducive, eventually, to identifying certain divine attributes and to the "gnosis regarding the divine."[130] The latter is about contemplating God the Logos as a creator and provident agent, culminating with the searching soul rejoicing in the divine fellowship.[131] And so, the stage-by-stage method of nature contemplation arrives at the knowledge the saints obtain in one go, so to speak, due to their enhanced abilities.

Athanasius does not explicitly connect the two approaches. It is very possible, however, that he considered introspection, that is, the first approach, central to the second one, the contemplation of the cosmos. The enhanced self of the first approach would then condition the successful grasp of reality through the second approach. If that is the case, then, from his viewpoint, knowing the self and knowing the universe intersect in the most creative and fulfilling of ways, excluding neither of these objects. His method heralds the New Copernican Turn that interests us here. However, while the contemplation of the self and the cosmos requires a method, Athanasius does not say it plainly.

More straightforward about the need for a contemplative method that includes rigorous research is Athanasius' predecessor, Clement.[132] His method has several layers, from existential to theoretical to practical. Clement is the first Christian author to have consistently affirmed the requirement of personal transformation through purification and virtue as a prerequisite for the great adventure of knowing, including knowing God, the universe, and the self.[133] This existential prerequisite entails a synergetic aspect, the contemplative ("gnostic") self reaching the highest knowledge due to divine proximity and enlightenment from above. But this requirement is not all there is to the method. Like Abraham and Moses—Clement's preferred scriptural paradigms—the contemplative self must also have an excellent grasp of curricular disciplines, including the available sciences, in order to apply appropriate tools to whatever objects are at hand.[134] By deploying these existential and intellectual tools, the self advances in knowledge and understanding, experiencing further transformations in so doing. Here, exploring the cosmos through mathematics and the sciences does not require circumventing the self. Likewise, the self asserts itself without ignoring the universe and the natural sciences.

To comprehend the cosmos, the self follows three steps, which can be described as analysis/description, interpretation/reflection, and vision (or the "gnostic" grasp of things). The first step amounts to *una scienza della natura*, as Laura Rizzerio has it, a genuine natural science[135] that includes theorising, experimenting, analysing, and synthesising information.[136] As a result of deploying these instruments, the self forms an accurate image of the physical world by the standards of the time. Without this image, no contemplation of nature is possible. Contemplation begins from established facts, not untested ideas and hearsay. As such, the contemplative self does not allow either the vastness of the cosmos or science to overwhelm itself. Through research and contemplation, the self embraces the status of an exile who thirsts to be at home in the universe. The point made earlier that the self's return might require learning mathematics and doing science originates here, in Clement's thinking.

The second step is about translating the scientifically acquired knowledge of the natural world in familiar categories. This corresponds to what we currently call science-engaged theology. Clement's audience was ecclesial. He communicated his sense of cosmic harmony through traditional tropes—scriptural and liturgical in nature—such as the psalm, the song, the orchestra, the musical instrument, and the choir.[137] Contemporary string theorists do the same, using a musical analogy known since at least Pythagoras, which resonates with musically educated people. In other words, the second, interpretative, step depends on the communicator's views, sensitivities, and audience. For example, McLeish suggests the rendition of the scientifically obtained view of reality into the language of poetry,[138] as well as of music.[139] Theology is a similar language that is familiar to people of faith. It undertakes to integrate the scientific description of reality, including cosmology, into the worldview of believers. The visual arts, furthermore, have been serving the theological engagement with the available sciences, as exemplified by the Byzantine and early modern Orthodox iconography of zodiacal motifs, depicting Christ as the centre of the universe (see Figure 4.2a—b). Of course, to render scientific information artistically, poetically, or theologically is no science; it is a way of popularising it, of assimilating it culturally and socially,[140] or, as Mark Flory would say, spiritually.[141] This, after all, is the primary task of science-engaged theology, at least as we use the concept throughout this book. And we believe that the successful completion of this task can help the self to find itself at home in the universe as cosmology and other sciences describe it.

Clement's third step can be called the vision of the saints or the divine vantage point. While the first two stages of the method are available to any seekers of the truth and can be learnt—the first one by scientists and science aficionados, the second one by science-engaged theologians and believers—the third one is reserved for the aristocrats of the spirit, the saints. In the latter case, knowing is not the outcome of research; it is a matter of being. Quality, or existential intensity, replaces quantity. Here, the self, divinely transformed, sees things divinely and from above, as it were, but not in a disconnected way. The transformed self is in direct touch with reality, with things as they are, as the *Popol Vuh*'s paradisal ancestors were. This is the kind of vision Columba had when he perceived the universe as a "single ray of the sun." In the same vein, Clement points out that, together with Christ and led by him, the saints comprehend what "the beings presently are, what the future things

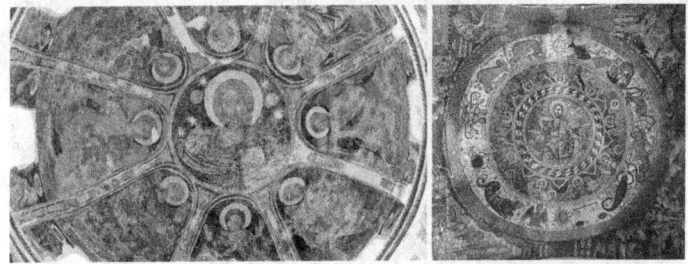

Figure 4.2a,b Byzantine celestial representations. The left-side image (Figure 4.2a) shows a Byzantine image of Christ surrounded by the sun, the moon, and stars against the backdrop of saints at Hagia Sophia Church, Mystras, fourteenth century.[142] The right-side image (Figure 4.2b) shows a seventeenth-century depiction of Christ as the centre of the visible and the invisible universe, represented by angels and the zodiacal signs, at Dekoulou Monastery in Mani.[143] The two images exemplify the interest of Orthodox Christians in interpreting the cosmos as Christ-centred.

will be, and how the things that have been brought into being have come to be."[144] This grasp of reality does not require mathematics, telescopes, or any other intellectual and technological tools. What makes it possible is the self's transformation in the presence of the divine. Here, the self rules supreme, but not as in Percy's mock transcendence via science and art. It rules in ways that far exceed our computations, dreams, models, and rationalisations.[145] Once it reaches this stage, the self knows because it is, like in Kazantzakis' "Cretan Glance," because it has realised its full potential. At this stage, the self has acquired, in Somerville's words, "deep respect for all life, in particular human life; and profound respect for the human spirit."[146]

In the light of the above, Clement proposes a contemplative method that links the educated, purified, and contemplative self, the sciences, the ecclesial mindset, the spiritual experience, and the world. This encompassing grasp of reality—richer than Percy's "tridimensional" relations or Nicolescu "ternary dialectic of reality"—presents the self and the universe as belonging together, as two sides of a much more complex whole.

In short, both Clement and Athanasius trained contemplative tools at the universe for the purposes of understanding it, part and whole. Overall, their interdisciplinary method corresponds to science-engaged theology, integrating the available scientific information into the self's quest to understand the world and its own place within it. This method, accordingly, straddles the natural sciences, the humanities, and theological insight—with the added bonus of not excluding either God or the self from the algorithms of reality and of knowing. Especially interesting is their shared point about transformed persons who attain wholeness and flourish and who find themselves at home within a cosmos that, while still mysterious, is neither irrational nor impossible to read. We are deliberately using the verb "to read" within this context, thinking of Paul Blowers' compelling argument for considering the traditional forms of nature contemplation analogues of spiritual hermeneutics—a cosmic *lectio divina*, as it were.[147] Evagrius Ponticus captures this idea by way of a dialogue between the famous hermit Antony of Egypt and an educated enquirer:

> One of the sages of that time came to righteous Antony, asking, "Father, how do you endure to be deprived of the consolation of books?" But he answered, "Philosopher, my book is the nature of created beings and it is in it that I wish to read about God's principles."[148]

The idea of reading nature is also featured in Athanasius, who writes: "Knowledge about God can be gained from visible things. By its order and harmony the creation signifies and proclaims its master and creator as though through letters."[149] He must have picked up the motif of the book of nature from Antony, whom he revered as a mentor. Back to Antony, his response, quoted just previously, sums up a whole theological theory of nature contemplation, including reading, which entails training and education, and insight, which denotes personal transformation. So equipped, the self, like Antony himself, grasps the divine principles of things, the rationality that undergirds the universe, finding knowledge as well as enjoyment. No trace here of either *sola scriptura* or the *tabula rasa* universe. Accordingly, Antony's reaction when he encountered beauty in the desert should not come as a surprise. As Athanasius tells us, the hermit travelled

> three days and three nights and arrived at a very high mountain. At the foothills of the mountain was water, clear, sweet, and quite cool. Downhill from there was flat land and a few struggling palms. Antony, as though God-inspired, fell in love with the place.[150]

Kazantzakis' Francis echoes the same kind of experience of peace and joy within the world—a world whose edges are tamed, which becomes meaningful, revealing itself as finely tuned, welcoming to the contemplative self.

The contemplation of nature, which in the previously mentioned patristic iterations includes the available natural sciences, appears to be the way ahead for the self's return, for the New Copernican Turn. But could this experience be replicated within the contemporary context? To answer this question, we have to visit more recent sources.

Modern Orthodox Literature

Orthodox literary accounts of holy life display a similar level of interest in nature contemplation, though without including the mediation of the sciences, not explicitly anyway. For example, the Russian Pilgrim refers to the impact of *philokalic* wisdom[151] upon the prayerful self's perception of nature in a new light:

> When with all this [i.e., the *Philokalia*'s wisdom] in mind I prayed with my heart, everything around me seemed delightful and marvellous. The trees, the grass, the birds, the earth, the air, the light seemed to be telling me that they existed for people's sake, that they witnessed to the love of God for humankind, that everything proved the love of God for humankind, that all things prayed to God and sang His praise.[152]

Far from changing the Pilgrim into a heartless person, obsessed with things transcendent and ethereal, or with the self considered in isolation from nature, the spiritual writings of the *Philokalia* opened his eyes towards the world. In that light, deciphered prayerfully, the world was replete with delight and meaning. And while the Pilgrim's prayer was not for the world, it seems, the *philokalic* perception of nature helped him to recognise nature's prayerful condition. Kazantzakis' Francis echoed this perception. The closing reference to a prayerful and praising creation evokes both the Book of Psalms and the patristic musical analogies mentioned above. The same appreciation for the world transpires once again in the Pilgrim's narrative:

> The prayer of my heart gave me such consolation that I felt there was no happier person on earth than I, and I doubted if there could be greater and fuller happiness in the kingdom of Heaven. Not only did I feel this in my own soul, but the whole outside world also seemed to me full of charm and delight. Everything drew me to love and thank God; people, trees, plants, animals. I saw them all as my kinsfolk, I found on all of them the magic of the Name of Jesus.[153]

There is no indication here of a structured method of nature contemplation, the way we find in Clement and, less clearly, in Athanasius. The Pilgrim's view of things is "from above," as it were, from the vantage point of pure prayer, which corresponds to Clement's "gnostic" insight of the saints. His view of things is not disconnected, however. Through the *philokalic* prayer, the Pilgrim's self found itself in the world and, together with it, in kinship with all things, which, similar to Antony's experience in the desert, caused enjoyment. This grasp of things is comprehensive, not reductionist, combining the view from above and the simple, immediate relish at the sight of things in nature. Either way, there is nothing bleak and terrifying here about the self's presence in the cosmos. The story of the Pilgrim evokes a paradisal kind of experience—or at least the psalmic doxology of the creation—but without Kazantzakis' idea of the responsibility of the self for the world around. That nuance, however, appears in the following example.

Fyodor Dostoevsky's Elder Zosima considers the environment along the lines of the *philokalic* Pilgrim's story[154] but adds the thought of human guardianship of the world. The point of departure is the conviction that God's Word loves all of the creation, not only humanity, and that the cosmos responds to this love: "the Word is for all creation, and every creature and every little leaf obeys the Word, singing the praises of God, weeping to Christ."[155] This perception is far remote from the angst Pascal's Western contemporaries experienced at the prospect of the infinite universe two centuries earlier. It is equally remote from the brute and mute nature of *sola scriptura* theology, which paved the way for Descartes' meaningless world of physicalist quantities. The self that wishes to rescue itself from insignificance and anxiety has to approach the world in Elder Zosima's manner. At some point, the latter urges his young disciple Alyosha Karamazov:

> Love God's creation, love every atom of it separately, and love it also as a whole; love every green leaf, every ray of God's light; love the animals and the plants and love every inanimate object. If you come to love all things, you will perceive God's mystery inherent in all things; once you

have perceived it, you will understand it better and better every day. And finally you will love the whole world with a total, universal love. Love the animals: God has given them the beginnings of thought and untroubled joy. So do not disturb their joy, do not torment them, do not deprive them of their wellbeing, do not work against God's intent. Man, do not pride yourself on your superiority to the animals, for they are without sin, while you, with all your greatness, you defile the earth wherever you appear and leave an ignoble trail behind you—and that is true, alas, for almost every one of us![156]

Contemplation of God's creation instructs the self in the ways of treating nature respectfully, gently, and lovingly and discloses the wisdom nature can, in turn, teach it, the self being the only anomalous thing in the universe. Contrary to the anthropocentric attempt at regaining significance, the self finds itself truly not by arrogant assertiveness and by despoiling nature but by appreciating the multitude of beings around it—from atoms to lifeforms—and by showing compassion to each and every one of them. Sensitivity to all things is what makes the world familiar to the self and gives it a sense of belonging. The reference to atoms, which are not part of the self's everyday experience, denotes the tacit acceptance of modern physics as revealing something significant about the world where the self journeys.

This contemplative and loving approach to things, doubled by insights from the natural sciences, facilitates more than the self's retrieval of itself. It gives it a deeper sense of the nature of reality. It makes it aware of a kind of quantum entanglement by which all things connect: "Everything is like the ocean, all things flow and are indirectly linked together, and if you push here, something will move at the other end of the world."[157] The sentence bespeaks global causality, the universe as an interactive open field. It anticipates Bohm's *holomovement* and *rheomode*, the idea of an "undivided wholeness in flowing movement."[158] This transformed perception, furthermore, makes possible the self's retrieval of its forgotten duty to change the world for the better. The insightful self does not seek to assert its dignity in a tyrannical fashion by doing violence to nature—by taking revenge on a nature that, for the last five hundred years, from *sola scriptura* to the infinite universe, it has been representing as strange to itself, oppressive, and mute. What rescues the self from insignificance is to know the truth of things; contemplation that includes scientific information about nature is instrumental to that end. And so, unlike Weinberg's grim view of reality, knowledge makes possible the self's contribution to the wellbeing of all things. Back to Kazantzakis, it is by "changing the eyes which see reality" that we "change reality."

One might wonder whether this wisdom can be applied to present circumstances. We would suggest that it can. Dostoevsky and Kazantzakis' practice of receptivity to—and mindfulness of—things around and distant from us is available to all, whether scientists, theologians, or anything else. Attentiveness to nature, integral to contemplation, requires practice but not specialised training, at least not in its traditional understanding.[159] In turn, Clement's method and its corollary, Athanasius' approach, are available only to educated seekers of truth, especially researchers, except for its last step. Having the advantage of incorporating scientific information, Clement's approach is quite appealing, and thus, we would suggest an excellent example of pursuing the goals of science-engaged theology. The same goes for Dostoevsky's inclusion of modern physics in Elder Zosima's nature contemplation at a grassroots level. But the last step of Clement's method, as much as the "from above" experience of Columba and the Russian Pilgrim, requires personal transformation. Nature contemplation is not of one piece, therefore, and the exiled self can choose whatever path of recovery suits itself.

The Contemporary Turn to Wonder and Contemplation

There is more good news for the self out there. An interesting new trend in scholarship focuses on the contemplation of nature, wonder, and awe as ways of making sense of things and of attaining personal wellbeing and joy in, or despite, this age of science and technology. The self can reconnect with the cosmos, both through the mediation of the sciences and directly. The discussion is ongoing.

For example, Sideris discerns between wonder at nature and wonder at our scientific representations of nature, and suggests that wonder at science can lead to people's separation from reality.[160] The sciences represent reality without being it; they work with abstract models, not with things. It is true that models are useful for understanding aspects of the universe. Nevertheless, within a culture that has abandoned the tridimensional symbolism of traditional societies, models circumvent complexity, the whole, including life, ecology, and the self. And scientific representations, or models, like the visual arts, count as expressions of human creativity that can lift the self "above the level of the farce," to paraphrase Weinberg once more. No wonder the self's fascination with them. That said, Sideris continues, when the self surrenders to the elegant coherence of scientific models, it loses touch with reality—as in the proverbial case of radio astronomers who peer into the depths of space shown by the screens of their computers but remain impassive to the beauty of the skies above their heads. Models or representations hinder the self's connection with nature, with the cosmos, the way urban lights deprive people of the sight of celestial vistas.[161] In this vein, as stargazers must put distance between themselves and light pollution, it takes a conscious effort to moderate our fascination for scientific models in order to experience reality directly, as our senses perceive it. Wonder at models, to continue Sideris' argument, is not conducive to finding a place for the self in the cosmos, but might alleviate the self's angst about cosmology's farsighted reach into the unknown.

In turn, Sideris, an environmental and religious studies scholar, points out that wonder at the world itself connects people with reality.[162] Her stance matches what we learnt from Dostoevsky, the Russian Pilgrim, and Kazantzakis. While astronomy can distract people from the splendour on high by crunching numbers that require expert checking and peer validation, looking up at the starry sky leads to awe and a sense of belonging. This direct experience with the world above and around us is available to all; it requires neither mathematics nor scientific expertise.[163] In Sideris' words, "cultivating . . . wonder through the senses . . . is something we can all do in some way."[164] We can go "beyond oneself," therefore, as children do, to "a kind of pleasurable, delightful state" where it becomes possible to "lose oneself in a completely enjoyable way."[165] Wonder and enjoyment improve the situation of the self in the world. They also pave the way for a theological perception of the universe. For believers, wonder is ultimately a matter of "thinking about God and God's creation . . . a kind of reverential feeling toward the Creator."[166] The authors whose thinking we reviewed in the previous sections would have appreciated these thoughts.

Sideris' overall attitude to science is both positive and nuanced. She believes that theologians and ethicists should take science seriously[167] and that "genuine wonder" supports scientific research. By "genuine wonder," she means a sustained and, most times, subjacent attentiveness to nature, doubled by curiosity about things.[168] However, against the triumphalist mythopoetic associated with scientific progress, she warns about taking it "*too seriously.*" The sciences, including cosmology, have limitations and experience impasses—such as the realisation that most of the universe eludes the current theories and physical measurements, discussed in Chapters Two and Three, or that scientific models sidetrack the self's efforts to reconnect with reality. A comprehensive worldview must balance scientific reductionism, the source of those impasses, and other ways of experiencing reality.[169] We have seen that, to an extent, this becomes a concern for the cosmologists who ponder the need for a new physics, one that might consider the significance of life and the self for nature's inner processes. Sideris gives the paradoxical example of Richard Dawkins, whose rationalism is tempered by a search for meaning through poetry and wonder.[170] The creative intersection of rigorous science and other forms of seeking to know are expressions of the self's return, and contemplation plays an important part in effecting it. It is on this note that we turn to other contemporary researchers of contemplative theory and practice.

For example, McLeish works from the other end of the spectrum. A physicist himself, he finds delight in science but emphasises the incompleteness of the scientific method as many scientists and enthusiasts currently picture it. Specifically, he takes exception to the widespread assumption of objectivity and discusses the importance of the subject, the contemplative self. In his Boyle Lecture 2021, McLeish advocates "the rediscovery of contemplation through science" in a manner that would have made Clement happy. He praises science for its achievements, but he invites it to a kind of conversion to accommodate the self and all of its faculties and experiences, foremost poetical imagination. And, McLeish continues, this existential conversion is the essence of science itself. To sustain its own impetus, it must rediscover and acknowledge "the unavoidably contemplative stage of constructing theoretical models of natural systems."[171] For contemplation is intrinsic to the scientific method, though most people forget about it. To that end, science will have to turn from the "illusion of perfect objectivity" to contemplation performed by human "subjects fully immersed in the world."[172] It would have to use the ternary lenses of Nicolescu, Percy, and Popper. In short, here, conversion amounts to humanising the sciences by abolishing the Cartesian rift between the subject and the object, or between self and nature, and between self and representations or models. In McLeish's words, this would take the following steps:

> Re-orienting science from the idolization of pure objectivity to a duality with immersed, incarnate subjectivity; from a false notion of pure rationality to a recognition of the partnership reason has always enjoyed with imagination; from an exclusive expertise to a shared participation, contemplation and joy; and from a convergent and prosaic narrative of the material world to an open, poetic, and infinitely beautiful one.[173]

This conversion, which entails science's change of relationship with the technology upon which it unilaterally depends, would include the self's many ways of perceiving reality and a holistic sense of nature as "being together."[174] This contemplative shift, in turn, would result in healing the self, human society, and the broken link between people and the physical world.[175] It would also open new avenues for creativity in science and other pursuits, such as theology and the "theology of science," as McLeish noted elsewhere.[176] The latter is what, throughout his book, we call science-engaged theology.

A similar though not identical path treads Bruce Foltz, who, drawing upon various "contemplative, poetic voices" of our times,[177] ponders the intersection of traditional approaches and perspectives available to us today. His goal is to return to a holistic, or noetic, apprehension of nature's mysteries that cause awe and enjoyment. This amounts to a "contemplation of nature that not only remains within the 'factical' but intensifies it, fulfills it, indeed radicalizes it."[178] The reader might remember Augustine's view of time intensified by the self's experience of it. In an early work, Foltz considers Heidegger's reinterpretation of nature—different from its objectified status in science and technology[179]—as a rich, polyvalent reality that ultimately reveals its status as sacred topography.[180] In this vein, Foltz explores forgotten nuances of nature as our home and contemplates our dwelling in the world as poetical, philosophical, and ethical agents who enhance its mystery and beauty.[181] But it is in more recent works that Foltz achieves a beautiful synthesis of ancient wisdom, Christian (and otherwise) contemplative approaches, and modern intellectual tools, including contemporary scientific culture. Here, the physical world is, for him, an open space of interaction, beauty, and meaning, where the subject and the object or the self and the cosmos intersect creatively, nurturing each other.[182] Here, environmentalism—with its determined and lucid crusade against the terrible impacts of objectivist and anthropocentric technoscience—retrieves "the warm heart of the contemplative soul,"[183] channeling its energies through the self, not around it. This is a full circle for the self and its quest for meaningful living in this world, which it explores in multiple ways but whose symbols it cherishes as inherent to its own constitution.

These examples, out of many more available, herald a new era of contemplative insight and comprehensiveness where the sciences and other forms of experiencing reality hold hands. These are signs of the New Copernican Turn, of retrieving the complex wholeness of human living in a world that no longer bears the scars of desertification inflicted upon it—or rather upon the self's perception of it—by supernaturalist representations, simplistic theologies, and reductionist scientific methodologies. As such, the self comes into its own vindicated and enriched, able to gaze into the unknown with wonder and love instead of fear and despair. Against this backdrop, yes, traditional forms of nature contemplation can be replicated within our own circumstances, namely, contemporary scientific culture, for the benefit of many, perhaps all.

Embracing the mystery of existence is apparently the common denominator of the various pursuits discussed in this chapter and the very opposite of the self's modern terror at the vastness of the universe. We might not know about the natural world as much as we thought we knew, and we clearly know much less about ourselves; Percy was right. Nevertheless, in the light of the above, there are ways within the horizons of mystery, of discovering ourselves in the crevices of so much unknowing—ways of bridging the self and the universe or, as Teilhard has it, "the Whole and the Person," which he considers the greatest achievement of *le phénomène chrétien*.[184] Here, incidentally, he gives expression to a core tenet of Orthodox Christianity, which conceives of the human experience with God *within* the cosmos, not only in history. More importantly, Teilhard and his intellectual progeny point to an alternative route, scientific as well as contemplative, for the self's estrangement in the modern universe of reductionist representations.

Are, then, contemplation and wonder hallmarks of the New Copernican Turn, the solution for the self's predicament and the way ahead for it to stop being "lost in the cosmos"? Are these the means by which people will be able to find themselves *and* the world or themselves *in* the world and to flourish in the world? Are these appropriate ways for cosmology to explore the greatest of its unknowns? We hope that they are, albeit in part. And even though the above proposal might upset certain cosmologists, for it sings a song that is still strange to them, we would also hope that one day, soon, they will realise that this new song is both the outcome and the fulfilment of what they are currently seeking—possibly the dawn of a new physics, one that bridges the gap between Descartes' "thinking thing" and "spaced thing," between the self and the cosmos.

Notes

1. For heliocentric thinking in antiquity, see Paul T. Keyser and Georgia L. Irby-Massie, eds., *The Encyclopedia of Ancient Natural Scientists: The Greek Tradition and Its Many Heirs* (London and New York: Routledge, 2008), esp. Henry Mendell's "Aristarkhos of Samos (ca 280–270 BCE)," 131–33, and Gábor Betegh's "Derveni papyrus (400–300 BCE?)," 242–43. For Copernicus' system and its impact, see Dennis Danielson, *Paradise Lost and the Cosmological Revolution* (Cambridge: Cambridge University Press, 2014), 51–77; Guy Freeland, "The Lamp in the Temple: Copernicus and the Demise of a Medieval Ecclesiastical Cosmology," in *1543 and All That*, 189–270, esp. 235–245; Arthur Koestler, *The Sleepwalkers: A History of Man's Changing Vision of the Universe* (New York: Macmillan, 1959), 119–99.
2. Percy, *Lost in the Cosmos*, 12.
3. Pascal, *Pensées*, 231.
4. Louth, *Discerning the Mystery*, 1–72.
5. Kurt Vonnegut, *The Sirens of Titan* (New York: Rosetta Books, 2000; ebook edn; 1st ed., 1959), 11.
6. Vonnegut, *The Sirens of Titan*, 12.
7. Weinberg, *The First Three Minutes*, 154–55.
8. Percy, *Lost in the Cosmos*, 133.
9. Vonnegut, *The Sirens of Titan*, 12.
10. Teilhard de Chardin, *Le phénomène humain*, 28.
11. Pascal, *Pensées*, 102, 233.
12. Hossenfelder, *Lost in Math* (ebook ed.), 180.
13. Vonnegut, *The Sirens of Titan*, 11.
14. Douglas Adams, *The Hitchhiker's Guide to the Galaxy*, ch. 8, in *The Ultimate Hitchhiker's Guide to the Galaxy* (London: Pan Books, 2020), 54.
15. See Lisa H. Sideris, "Wonder Sustained: A Reply to Critics," *Zygon* 54, no. 2 (2019): 1–28, esp. 7–9.
16. Percy, *Lost in the Cosmos*, 174–204.
17. Percy, *Lost in the Cosmos*, 54. Cf. Sideris, "Wonder Sustained," 3.
18. Percy, *Lost in the Cosmos*, 288.
19. Percy, *Lost in the Cosmos*, 289–91.
20. Percy, *Lost in the Cosmos*, 127.
21. Percy, *Lost in the Cosmos*, 12.
22. See La Matina, "On Subjects," 111–16.
23. Percy, *Lost in the Cosmos*, 18.

24 See Neil et al., *Dreams, Virtue and Divine Knowledge*, and the contributions to *Ancient Philosophy of the Self*, ed. Pauliina Remes and Juha Sihvola, The New Synthese Historical Library 64 (Springer, 2008).
25 For metaphysics as a discourse on the self in the fourth century, see Costache, *Humankind and the Cosmos*, 147–53, 210–18; Doru Costache, "A Note on Evagrius' Cosmological and Metaphysical Statements," *The Journal of Theological Studies* 71, no. 2 (2020): 718–30, esp. 725–29.
26 Pascal, *Pensées* 231.
27 Descartes, *Discourse on the Method*, 4. Further up the corridors of cultural history, his distinction amounts to a creative iteration—via the Platonic tradition of interiority—of Aristotle's methodological distinction between science and ethics, as well as the related distinction between theoretical and applied disciplines. See on this the fairly recent edited collection of essays, *Bridging the Gap between Aristotle's Science and Ethics*, ed. Devin Henry and Karen Margarethe Nielsen (Cambridge: Cambridge University Press, 2015).
28 Pascal, *Pensées*, 145.
29 For Archimedes as an inspiration for Pascal's generation, see Jocelyn Holland and Edgar Landgraf, "The Archimedean Point: From Fixed Positions to the Limits of Theory," *SubStance* 43, no. 3 (2014): 3–11.
30 See William Shatner, "My Trip to Space Made Me Realise We Have Only One Earth—It Must Live Long and Prosper," *The Guardian*, December 7, 2022, accessed 10 February 2024, https://tinyurl.com/53x45fz5.
31 Mircea Eliade, *The Sacred and the Profane: The Nature of Religion*, trans. Willard R. Trask (New York: Harcourt, 1959), 43–44, 80, 105, 167–72, 203–95.
32 Athanasius, *On the Incarnation*, 41. The same goes for his younger colleagues, Gregory of Nyssa and John Chrysostom. See references and detailed analyses in Costache, *Humankind and the Cosmos*, 329–64.
33 Karl Popper, *In Search of a Better World: Lectures and Essays from Thirty Years*, trans. Laura J. Bennett (London and New York: Routledge, 1994), 7–9, 20–27; Karl Popper, *Knowledge and the Mind-Body Problem: In Defence of Interaction* (London and New York: Routledge, 1994), 5–10, 24–34.
34 Basarab Nicolescu, *From Modernity to Cosmodernity: Science, Culture, and Spirituality*, SUNY Series in Western Esoteric Traditions (New York: State University of New York Press, 2014), 128–30. For similar views about scientific reductionism, dubbed "a false model of nature," see David Bentley Hart, "Science and Theology: Where the Consonance Really Lies," *After Science and Religion*, 61–74, esp. 67–72.
35 Percy, *Lost in the Cosmos*, 156–57.
36 Percy, *Lost in the Cosmos*, 147–48.
37 Adam Frank, "Science Claims a 'God's-Eye View' of Reality. This Is Fiction," *Big Think* (June 8, 2023), accessed June 27, 2023, http://tinyurl.com/5n6bksbv.

38 Percy, *Lost in the Cosmos*, 258–68. For recent deconstructions of objectivism, see Mark W. Flory, "The Standpoint of Transformativity: Re-envisioning Science, Nature, and the Self," in *Seeing and Being Seen: Aesthetics and Environmental Philosophy*, ed. Joshua Coleman (Hamilton Books, 2017), 58–68, esp. 65–88; Tom McLeish, "The Rediscovery of Contemplation through Science," *Zygon* 56, no. 3 (2021): 758–76, esp. 760–61, 766, 774, https://doi.org/10.1111/zygo.12719.
39 Frank, "Science."
40 Percy, *Lost in the Cosmos*, 287.
41 Percy, *Lost in the Cosmos*, 133, 173, 174 etc. While the sciences are the self's way of exploring nature, they are not nature; they are its representations. Likewise, the self's theology, philosophy, and arts are nature's representations, not nature itself. See Nesteruk, *The Sense of the Universe*, 255–304.
42 McLeish, "The Rediscovery of Contemplation," 2, 4–5.
43 Teilhard de Chardin, *Le phénomène humain*, 51.
44 Percy, *Lost in the Cosmos*, 260.
45 Margaret Somerville, *The Ethical Imagination: Journeys of the Human Spirit*, The Massey Lectures (Toronto, ON: Anansi, 2006; ebook ed.), 9.
46 Nicolescu, *From Modernity to Cosmodernity*, 15.
47 Percy, *Lost in the Cosmos*, 158, 161.
48 Stăniloae, *Teologia dogmatică ortodoxă*, 1: 359–60; 1: 366–74; Stăniloae, *Iisus Hristos, lumina lumii şi îndumnezeitorul omului* (Jesus Christ, light of the world and deifier of humankind) (Bucureşti: Anastasia, 1993), 28. See also Costache, "One Description," 34.
49 Foltz, *The Noetics of Nature*, 138–46.
50 For a summary of anthropic ideas, see Nicolescu, *From Modernity to Cosmodernity*, 92–95. See also the classical work of Barrow and Tipler, *The Anthropic Cosmological Principle*.
51 Percy, *Lost in the Cosmos*, 26.
52 Adams, *The Hitchhiker's Guide to the Galaxy*, ch. 9 (at 56).
53 In his words, "coextensive with their Outside (*Dehors*), there is an Inside (*Dedans*) of Things" (Teilhard de Chardin, *Le phénomène humain*, 53).
54 H. P. Lovecraft, "Supernatural Horror in Literature" (originally published in 1927 and revised in 1934), in *The Fiction: Complete and Unabridged* (New York: Barnes & Noble, 2008), 1042.
55 Penrose, *The Emperor's New Mind*, 50, 66, 82, 85, 216–17 etc.
56 Penrose, *The Emperor's New Mind*, 170.
57 Penrose, *The Emperor's New Mind*, 172–73. In the same vein, Hossenfelder doubts that we can be "on par with nature, able to look at the universe and say, 'I understand'." See Hossenfelder, *Lost in Math*, 153.
58 Hossenfelder, *Lost in Math*, ch. 1.
59 Hossenfelder, *Lost in Math*, 148, 152.
60 Percy, *Lost in the Cosmos*, 126–34, 188–94.
61 Jack Dempsey, "Cosmos Erotica: The Shapes of Minoan Desire," January 28, 2011, accessed December 10, 2023, http://tinyurl.com/3tjpaxjt.

62 See Jean Clottes, *What Is Paleolithic Art: Cave Paintings and the Dawn of Human Creativity*, trans. Oliver Y. Martin and Robert D. Martin (Chicago, IL and London: University of Chicago Press, 2016); Duane Hamacher et al., *The First Astronomers: How Indigenous Elders Read the Stars* (Sydney and Melbourne: Allen & Unwin, 2022); Diane Johnson, *Night Skies of Aboriginal Australia: A Noctuary* (Sydney: Sydney University Press, 2014).
63 Abba Poemen, saying 191, in *The Sayings of the Desert Fathers: The Alphabetic Collection*, trans. Benedicta Ward, Cistercian Studies 59 (Kalamazoo: Cistercian Publications, 1975). See also, in the same collection, Andrew 1; Evagrius 7; Longinus 1; Poemen 62.
64 Credit: The University of Sydney Library's Rare Books and Special Collections. Call number: Dewey 936.4 113, accessed March 20, 2024, https://tinyurl.com/3d6vpd8m.
65 Donald H. Rumsfeld, "DoD News Briefing," U. S. Department of Defense, 12 February 2002, accessed 20 February 2023, http://tinyurl.com/4apf6zb6.
66 Lucian Blaga, *Trilogia cunoașterii* (knowledge trilogy) (București: Humanitas, 2013), 112–13.
67 Blaga, *Trilogia cunoașterii*, 158.
68 Blaga, *Trilogia cunoașterii*, 159–69, 201–08, 222–43.
69 Lucian Blaga, "Eu nu strivesc corola de minuni a lumii," in *Poemele luminii* (poems of light) (Sibiu: Cosînzeana, 1919).
70 See Margaret Somerville, "Could 'The Wonder Equation' Help Us to Be More Ethical? A Personal Reflection," *Ethics & Behavior* 32, no. 3 (2022): 226–40, esp. 231–32, 237–38, https://doi.org/10.1080/1050842 2.2020.1867861.
71 Somerville, "The Wonder Equation," 237.
72 Percy, *Lost in the Cosmos*, 130. For Tom McLeish, *Faith and Wisdom in Science* (Oxford: Oxford University Press, 2014), 190–96; it all begins with daring to ask difficult questions.
73 Pascal, *Pensées* 232.
74 Percy, *Lost in the Cosmos*, 127.
75 Vonnegut, *The Sirens of Titan*, 12.
76 "Our entire dignity consists in thinking. It is from there that we should begin to rise, not from space and duration" (Pascal, *Pensées*, 232).
77 Bohm, *Wholeness*, 68–79; David Bohm, "A New Theory of the Relationship of Mind and Matter," *Philosophical Psychology* 3, no. 2 (1990): 271–86, esp. 281–85, https://doi.org/10.1080/09515089008573004. See Grijs and Costache, "The Cosmology of David Bohm," 210, 216.
78 Nesteruk, *The Sense of the Universe*, 87–118.
79 See "the World's internal face comes to light on the level of our human consciousness, gazing upon itself as though in a mirror" (Teilhard de Chardin, *Le phénomène humain*, 60). Teilhard considers cosmic evolution integral to a process of universal humanisation, with humankind representing "the transitional climax of an Anthropogenesis that itself crowns a Cosmogenesis" (*Le phénomène humain*, 28).

80 Nesteruk, *The Sense of the Universe*, 82.
81 Gregory the Theologian, *Oration* 38.321–324.
82 Maximus, *Difficulties* 41.3–9. See Costache, "Mapping Reality," 381–90; Louth, "Man and Cosmos," 60–62.
83 See Louth, "Man and Cosmos," 69–70.
84 Carl Sagan, *Contact* (New York: Gallery Books, 2019), 372.
85 Somerville, *The Ethical Imagination*, 15.
86 Wagner and Briggs, *The Penultimate Curiosity*, 110.
87 See Doru Costache, "Abraham, the Contemplation of Nature, and Divine Vision in Clement of Alexandria," in *Knowing God in Light: Theophany and Language*, ed. Nichifor Tănase, Marius Portaru, and Daniel Lemeni (Berlin: LIT Verlag, forthcoming).
88 Barrow, *The Origin of the Universe*, 45.
89 Davies, *The Mind of God*, 21.
90 Gregory of Nyssa, *An Apology of the Hexameron* 10.
91 Gregory of Nyssa, *On the Constitution of the Human Being* (in *On the Human Image of God*) 8.5.145.
92 See Jean Clottes, "The Paleolithic Cave Art of France," accessed March 10, 2024, www.bradshawfoundation.com/clottes/index.php.
93 See Bohm, "A New Theory," 271–75, 281–85; Penrose, *The Emperor's New Mind*, 405–50 (ch. "Where lies the physics of mind?"); Penrose, *The Road to Reality*, 1030–33 (ch. "The Roles of Mentality in Physical Theory"); Stapp, *Mindful Universe*, 119–38 (ch. "Consciousness and the Anthropic Questions"). See also the relevant essays in *Consciousness and the Universe: Quantum Physics, Evolution, Brain & Mind*, ed. Roger Penrose and Stuart Hameroff (Cosmology Science Publishers, 2011).
94 La Matina, "On Subjects," 111–18, 145–48.
95 Marcello La Matina, "The State of Things to Come: The Notion of Truth between Contemporary Philosophy of Language and Fourth-Century Eastern Patristics," *Blityri* 11:1–2 (2022): 97–118, esp. 105–08, 114–15.
96 Koestler, *The Sleepwalkers*, 520–24.
97 Bruce V. Foltz, *Byzantine Incursions on the Borders of Philosophy: Contesting the Boundaries of Nature, Art, and Religion* (Cham: Springer, 2019), 99.
98 Nikos Kazantzakis, *Report to Greco*, trans. P. A. Bien (Simon and Schuster, 2012; ebook edn), ch. 3.
99 Kazantzakis, *Report to Greco*, ch. 31.
100 Nikos Kazantzakis, *Saint Francis*, trans. P. A. Bien, Loyola Classics (Chicago: Loyola Press, 1962; ebook ed.), 29.
101 This to and fro possibly echoes Clement of Alexandria's Abraham on his way to the mountain, when he took in the beauty of the world as pointing to the ineffable zone of God's dwelling. See Clement, *Stromateis* 5.11.73.2–3. For an analysis of this passage, see Costache, *Humankind and the Cosmos*, 123–26.
102 Acts 17:28 (NRSV).
103 Kazantzakis, *Saint Francis*, 30. Here, Kazantzakis echoes the very endearing characterisation of God as "Holy Father" in Francis' "Parchment Given to Brother Leo" and the absence of the word "God" from

his "Canticle of Brother Sun." See *Francis and Clare: The Complete Works*, trans. Regis J. Armstrong and Ignatius C. Brady, The Classics of Western Spirituality (New York: Paulist Press, 1982), 38–39, 99–100.
104 Kazantzakis, *Saint Francis*, 63–64.
105 See Bruce V. Foltz, "Traces of Divine Fragrance, Droplets of Divine Love: On the Beauty of Visible Creation," and John Anthony McGuckin, "The Beauty of the World and Its Significance in St. Gregory the Theologian," in *Toward an Ecology of Transfiguration*, 324–36, 34–45.
106 Kazantzakis, *Saint Francis*, 3 (prologue).
107 For analyses of relevant patristic sources, see Costache's *Humankind and the Cosmos*, 27–60, 329–64; "John Moschus on Asceticism and the Environment," *Colloquium* 48, no. 1 (2016): 21–34; "Mapping Reality," 381–85. For a relevant overview of modern Orthodox theologians, see Theokritoff, "Creator and Creation," 70–73, 74–75.
108 See Tolkien, *The Lord of the Rings*, 85.
109 Athanasius, *Against the Gentiles* 30–34.
110 Athanasius, *Against the Gentiles* 2, 35–44.
111 For Athanasius' epistemology, see David Bradshaw, "Introduction," in *Natural Theology in the Eastern Orthodox Tradition*, 8–13; Costache, *Humankind and the Cosmos*, 171–86; Neil et al., *Dreams, Virtue and Divine Knowledge*, 100–13.
112 Especially obvious in Athanasius, *Against the Gentiles* 2.
113 Athanasius, *Against the Gentiles* 30, 33. For these elements within the broader Christian tradition, see Foltz, *The Noetics of Nature*, 11–12.
114 Vonnegut, *The Sirens of Titan*, 11.
115 David Brakke, *Demons and the Making of the Monk: Spiritual Combat in Early Christianity* (Cambridge, MA, and London: Harvard University Press, 2006), 44; David Brakke, *Athanasius and the Politics of Asceticism*, Oxford Early Christian Studies (Oxford: Clarendon Press, 1995), 239–40.
116 See Athanasius, *On Sickness and Health* 8.6–7. See on this Neil et al., *Dreams*, 88–90.
117 See Khaled Anatolios, *Athanasius: The Coherence of His Thought* (London and New York: Routledge, 1998), 34–35. For a similar point in regard to Maximus the Confessor, see Louth, "Man and Cosmos," 69.
118 See Adomnán of Iona, *Life of St Columba* 1.1,35.
119 *Popol Vuh* 4.
120 Evagrius, *On Thoughts* (*Sur les pensées*) 39. See on this Augustine Casiday, *Reconstructing the Theology of Evagrius Ponticus: Beyond Heresy* (Cambridge: Cambridge University Press, 2013), 180–83.
121 Pseudo-Macarius, *The Fifty Spiritual Homilies* 1.2. For illustrations of this experience, see Costache, "Adam's Holiness," 334–39.
122 E. P. Meijering, *Orthodoxy and Platonism in Athanasius: Synthesis or Antithesis?* reprint with corrections (Leiden: Brill, 1974), 8–9.
123 Athanasius, *Against the Gentiles* 2.
124 See Costache, *Humankind and the Cosmos*, 173–74.
125 Athanasius, *Against the Gentiles* 2.
126 Athanasius, *Against the Gentiles* 41.

127 See Anatolios, *Athanasius*, 48–50.
128 Athanasius, *Against the Gentiles* 38, 43. See Costache, *Humankind and the Cosmos*, 98–106.
129 Athanasius, *Against the Gentiles* 2, 41.
130 Athanasius, *Against the Gentiles* 2.
131 Athanasius, *Against the Gentiles* 2. See Costache, *Humankind and the Cosmos*, 172–86.
132 For Clement's method, see Bradshaw, "Introduction," 4–8; Costache, *Humankind and the Cosmos*, 115–36; Havrda, *The So-Called Eighth Stromateus*, 27–28, 34–73.
133 Clement, *Stromateis* 4.25.161; 5.3.17; 5.12.82; 5.13.83; 6.7.60; 6.18.166. See Costache, *Humankind and the Cosmos*, 117–19.
134 Clement, *Stromateis* 1.5.32; 6.10.80; 6.11.90. See Costache, *Humankind and the Cosmos*, 120–28.
135 Laura Rizzerio, *Clemente di Alessandria e la "φυσιολογία veramente gnostica": Saggio sulle origini e le implicazioni di un'epistemologia e di un'ontologia 'cristiane'* (Leuven: Peeters, 1996), 98, and the whole chapter on "physiology" (natural science), 39–99.
136 Clement, *Stromateis* 2.17.76. These steps coincide with Platonic science. Luc Brisson, "Plato's Natural Philosophy and Metaphysics," in *A Companion to Ancient Philosophy*, ed. Mary Louise Gill and Pierre Pellegrin, Blackwell Companions to Philosophy (Oxford: Blackwell Publishing, 2006), 212–31, 215–16.
137 Clement, *Exhortation* 1.2.4; 1.4.4; 1.6.1; 1.6.5; 1.7.3. See Costache, *Humankind and the Cosmos*, 82–96.
138 McLeish, "The Rediscovery of Contemplation," 10–17.
139 See Tom McLeish, *The Poetry and Music of Science: Comparing Creativity in Science and Art* (Oxford: Oxford University Press, 2019), 191–260.
140 See Costache, *Humankind and the Cosmos*, 131–33.
141 Flory, "The Standpoint of Transformativity," 58–68.
142 Credit: Wikimedia Commons, accessed 15 February 2024, https://tinyurl.com/jyzrr8z3.
143 Credit: Nikos Tsivikis, 2022. We are grateful to Dr Tsivikis for the permission to use his photo here.
144 Clement, *Stromateis* 6.9.78.
145 See Costache, *Humankind and the Cosmos*, 133–35.
146 Somerville, *The Ethical Imagination*, 6.
147 See Blowers, *Drama of the Divine Economy*, 315–35.
148 Evagrius, *The Monk* 92. See Costache, *Humankind and the Cosmos*, 208–10.
149 Athanasius, *Against the Gentiles* 34. See Costache, *Humankind and the Cosmos*, 181–83.
150 Athanasius, *Life of Antony* 49–50. For analyses of this passage against the backdrop of ascetic literature, see John Chryssavgis, *In the Heart of the Desert: The Spirituality of the Desert Fathers and Mothers* (Bloomington, IN: World Wisdom, 2003), 85–87; Andrew Mellas, "The Chora Within: Unveiling Asceticism in St Athanasius' *Life of St Antony*," in

Alexandrian Legacy: A Critical Appraisal, ed. Doru Costache, Philip Kariatlis, and Mario Baghos (Newcastle upon Tyne: Cambridge Scholars, 2015), 122–38, esp. 135, 137–38.

151 For a historical introduction to the *Philokalia*, see John Anthony McGuckin, "The Making of the *Philokalia*: A Tale of Monks and Manuscripts," in *The* Philokalia*: A Classic Text of Orthodox Spirituality*, ed. Brock Bingaman and Bradley Nassif (Oxford University Press, 2012), 36–49. For a summary of *philokalic* theology, see Andrew Louth, "The Theology of the *Philokalia*," in *Abba: The Tradition of Orthodoxy in the West*, ed. John Behr, Andrew Louth, and Dimitri Conomos (Crestwood, NY: St Vladimir's Seminary Press, 2003), 351–61. For the impact of the *Philokalia* upon the Russian Pilgrim, see Andrew Louth, *Modern Orthodox Thinkers: From the* Philokalia *to the Present* (London: Society for Promoting Christian Knowledge, 2015), 11.

152 *The Way of a Pilgrim and the Pilgrim Continues His Way*, trans. R. M. French (London: The Society for Promoting Christian Knowledge, 1996), 46 (slightly altered). For a brief analysis of this passage, see Foltz, "Traces of Divine Fragrance," 330.

153 *The Way of a Pilgrim*, 119.

154 For the impact of the *Philokalia* on Dostoevsky, see Louth, *Modern Orthodox Thinkers*, 5–6.

155 Dostoevsky, *The Brothers Karamazov*, 504. See Foltz, *The Noetics of Nature*, 149–53 and "Traces of Divine Fragrance," 330.

156 Dostoevsky, *The Brothers Karamazov*, 547 (slightly altered).

157 Dostoevsky, *The Brothers Karamazov*, 548.

158 Bohm, *Wholeness*, xiv, 14, 190–97; Bohm, "A New Theory," 273.

159 See John M. Cooper, *Pursuits of Wisdom: Six Ways of Life in Ancient Philosophy from Socrates to Plotinus* (Princeton, NJ and Oxford: Princeton University Press, 2012), 340–41, 364; Pierre Hadot, *Philosophy as a Way of Life: Spiritual Exercises from Socrates to Foucault*, trans. Michael Chase (Oxford: Blackwell, 1995), 59, 85, 130, 243–44.

160 Lisa H. Sideris, "Is Wonder at the Scientific Enterprise Good for Us, and for Our Relationship to the Natural World?" *Annals of the New York Academy of Sciences* 1501, no. 1 (2021): 67–74, esp. 68–73, https://doi.org/10.1111/nyas.14490. See also Lisa H. Sideris, *Consecrating Science: Wonder, Knowledge, and the Natural World* (Berkeley, CA: University of California Press, 2017), 22–25.

161 See Johan Eklöf, *The Darkness Manifesto: On Light Pollution, Night Ecology, and the Ancient Rhythms That Sustain Life*, trans. Elizabeth DeNoma (New York: Scribner, 2024).

162 Steve Paulson, Lisa Sideris, Jennifer Stellar, and Piercarlo Valdesolo, "Beyond Oneself: The Ethics and Psychology of Awe," *Annals of the New York Academy of Sciences* 1501, no. 1 (2021): 30–47, esp. 35, doi: 10.1111/nyas.14323.

163 Sideris, *Consecrating Science*, 14–28; "Wonder Sustained," 4–6.

164 Paulson and Sideris, "Beyond Oneself," 35. See also Sideris, "Wonder at the Scientific Enterprise," 69–70. This view corresponds to McLeish's position against the professionalisation of wonder and contemplation in

165 Paulson and Sideris, "Beyond Oneself," 32.
166 Paulson and Sideris, "Beyond Oneself," 33.
167 Sideris, *Consecrating Science*, 1, 6–7. The same goes for Somerville, *The Ethical Imagination*, 9–10.
168 Lisa Sideris, "To Benefit from Wonder, Make Sure You've Got the Genuine Kind," *Psyche* (October 4, 2022), accessed December 20, 2023, https://tinyurl.com/yj4efddj.
169 Sideris, *Consecrating Science*, 2–3.
170 Sideris, *Consecrating Science*, 29–49.
171 McLeish, "The Rediscovery of Contemplation," 763.
172 McLeish, "The Rediscovery of Contemplation," 759.
173 McLeish, "The Rediscovery of Contemplation," 774–75. Elsewhere, he speaks of science's alliance with such subjective and comprehensive emotions and experiences as love. See McLeish, *Faith and Wisdom*, 196–207. For a very similar stance, see Somerville, *The Ethical Imagination*, 10–14.
174 McLeish, "The Rediscovery of Contemplation," 761.
175 McLeish, *Faith and Wisdom*, 151, 208, 210, 212, 241–48.
176 McLeish, *The Poetry and Music of Science*, 295–97, 312–15; Tom McLeish, "Before Science and Religion: Learning from Medieval Physics," *Modern Believing* 62, no. 2 (2021): 124–35, https://doi.org/10.3828/mb.2021.9.
177 Foltz, *The Noetics of Nature*, xii, 63–73, 88–111.
178 Foltz, *The Noetics of Nature*, 20; see also 3–6. Cf. Bruce V. Foltz, "'The Lord Is in this Place, Yet I Did Not See It': From the Concept of Nature to the Experience of Creation," in *Orthodox Christianity and Modern Science: Theological, Philosophical, Scientific and Historical Aspects of the Dialogue*, 121–39, esp. 132–38; Foltz, *Byzantine Incursions*, 37–38, 103. See also Knight, *Eastern Orthodoxy*, 8, 11, 14, 16, 51.
179 Bruce V. Foltz, *Inhabiting the Earth: Heidegger, Environmental Ethics, and the Metaphysics of Nature* (NJ: Humanities Press, 1995), 63–108, 141–42.
180 Foltz, *Inhabiting the Earth*, 130–40, 143–53.
181 Foltz, *Inhabiting the Earth*, 154–80.
182 See Foltz, *The Noetics of Nature* and *Byzantine Incursions*.
183 Foltz, *Byzantine Incursions*, 101.
184 Teilhard de Chardin, *Le phénomène humain*, 324–25. At 331, he concludes: "It is it [the Christian phenomenon] and only it that, in the modern world, shows the capacity to synthesise in a single vital act the Whole and the Person."

5 Conclusions

This book began by discussing the universe's knowns and unknowns from the viewpoints of contemporary cosmology and the Orthodox Christian tradition, proposing an exercise in science-engaged theology. It then turned to the greatest of unknowns, the destiny of the self in the universe, highlighting the existential ramifications of combining recent developments within cosmology with traditional forms of nature contemplation. The goals of this exercise are diverse, from summarising scientific information for the benefit of theologians and philosophers to showcasing Orthodox Christian theology's aptitude for engaging the sciences, foremost cosmology, to pointing out the signs of a New Copernican Turn in regard to bridging the self and the universe. Several reasons undergird this endeavour.

What makes this undertaking possible is the fact that theology, in its pursuit of the truth, gathers it not only from what belongs to God but also from Caesar's world, to paraphrase a famous passage.[1] This is especially true about what Henri Crouzel called *théologie en recherche* or *théologie en exercice*, the theology that seeks understanding by engaging various disciplines.[2] It is also true that major early Christian authors, whose wisdom is of the essence for Orthodox theology, asserted the priority of faith-based worldviews when it comes to believers. That said, they did not disparage the available sciences either and, in fact, encouraged the seekers of truth to explore them.[3] To draw water from various wellsprings was integral to theology's mandate from the outset. We discovered that, from its patristic origins and for many centuries, Orthodox theology was interested in making sense of reality including by engaging the sciences. This presupposes an unusual interest in the shifting scientific paradigms throughout history. McLeish's point that "the *theological consequences* of the ability of humans to do science are profound and beautiful"[4] captures this interest well. And we hope that readers have gleaned relevant consequences from the previous analysis.

Against this historical backdrop, we then suggested that, being equipped for this task, Orthodox theology should continue to engage the contemporary scientific culture, including cosmology, even if merely for the purposes of better communicating its wisdom in this age of science. Accordingly, we established that scientific information—with Chapter Two providing a rigorous account to that end—is instrumental towards the articulation of a theological worldview of consequence today. In the course of our analysis, we discovered that theology should do so for at least two other reasons of broader relevance. It is by considering these reasons that we exemplify the workings of Orthodox theology when it comes to engaging contemporary cosmology.

Thus, given the keen interest of early Christian and medieval thinkers in grasping the nature of reality, first, theology should engage cosmology in order to facilitate a better understanding of the universe by the community it serves. We have not discussed what prompted this lasting interest of the Orthodox in making sense of things, but this is a documented fact. From the early days of Christianity on, believers' worldview included the natural world, not only culture, the values, and the built environment.[5] More important for our purposes here is that theology cannot communicate with educated audiences by cultural references to a bygone era, namely, by relying on ancient and medieval knowledge to describe the universe. It is primarily in order to reach out to contemporary audiences that theology has to engage the scientific culture of our time, primarily cosmology, which makes believers aware of the universe as we understand it today, with its many knowns and many more unknowns. As we have seen throughout this book, science-engaged theology is not about replacing scientific facts with theological representations of reality. Nor is it about adding theological correctives to the sciences. It is about including established scientific facts into the worldview of faith communities and assisting those communities to process scientific information in ways that are relevant to them. In this vein, Chapter Three outlines several aspects of contemporary cosmology that can be considered, very profitably, together with patristic ideas about the universe, such as its dynamic, evolutionary nature. It also gives examples of modern Orthodox theologians who had undertaken to do just that, namely, engaging aspects of contemporary cosmology conducive to a deeper understanding of the Christian worldview, such as the natural mortality of the universe and of everything within it.

The second reason for engaging cosmology is the need to help rescue the self from being "lost in the cosmos." This is a matter of critical importance, at least when we consider the psychoses generated by the perspective of an infinite and pointless universe. And although we did not discuss this issue at length here, neither of us being a psychologist, the significance of our findings for mapping this phenomenon should be obvious—at least through the mediation of Walker Percy's insightful book, which has guided us throughout.

What we did, however, was seek the causes of the self's modern angst, discovering that the perspective of an infinite universe was not the only factor at play. It is true that, as Chapter Four posits, awareness of the boundless cosmos triggered a strong emotional response in Pascal's generation, whose aftershocks are still felt more subconsciously than otherwise. Nevertheless, what left that generation and the following ones bereft of means to withstand the shock of infinity was an earlier development. It was the introduction of a new theological idea, *sola scriptura*, namely, that God speaks only through written words, not also through the meaningfulness of the cosmos. This idea was without precedent during the first millennium and a half of Christian theology, absent from scriptural accounts, and remains foreign to the Orthodox mindset. The consequences of this theological novelty found expression in the thinking of Pascal's contemporary, Descartes, who considered the universe a "spaced thing" void of qualitative significance and theological meaning. It is this novelty that left the self without geodesics in the world. No wonder the arrival of the infinite universe and its staggering, incomprehensible numbers found the self weakened and reduced to a thinking, anxious reed. Chapter Four dealt with these matters within their context.

It proposed, furthermore, a layered solution for overcoming the self's predicament from the viewpoint of the Orthodox tradition in conversation with similar developments in other cultures, including recent developments in physics and cosmology. At the centre of this solution resides the theory and practice of nature contemplation, which, in more sophisticated iterations, makes recourse to scientific information while it remains available to the self that has no scientific inclinations. The outcome of contemplation, either way, is the self's retrieval of its sense of belonging and purpose within a theologically meaningful universe. This outcome gestures towards what, throughout this book, we called a New Copernican Turn.

Another important outcome of our research was realising that, together with its traditional openness to science, what makes possible Orthodox theology's engagement of contemporary cosmology is the latter's humble acknowledgment of falling short of understanding the universe. Specifically, after decades of tremendous research, cosmologists discovered the vastness of the unknown ahead of us, with the estimates pointing to ninety-five per cent of the universe eluding the current models and observations. The universe is more mysterious today than it has ever been.[6] It is at least at this juncture that cosmology, even that which is described by atheist scientists, and Orthodox theology could meet since both treat the cosmos apophatically, in theological parlance. And while to realise the extent of the unknown is a good reason for pursuing cosmological research further, we showed that to do so we might need a new physics—perhaps one that integrates the self as a fundamental ingredient of reality, even without the traditional theory and practice of nature contemplation having anything to do about it. This would amount to a genuine New Copernican Turn for contemporary science and culture.

Incidentally, we have seen that Orthodox theology, while not claiming scientific competence, points to possible aspects of this new physics and cultivates alternate ways of perceiving reality, such as insight, wonder, and contemplative practices, which allow it to represent reality as emerging at the nexus of the self and the universe. These ways of perceiving nature, of course, cannot be considered scientific by the current standards of methodological naturalism, regardless of how surprising their outcomes might be. But a comprehensive cosmology that accommodates the self, or consciousness, might need cooperation across more points of view than purely scientific ones. Perhaps theology's scientific engagement could one day receive a response from cosmology's theological or philosophical engagement. We hope that this book provides useful hints to that end, though not advice. After all, as Tolkien says, "advice is a dangerous gift, even from the wise to the wise, and all courses may run ill."[7]

Nobody can anticipate how things will turn out, in the long run, for either science-engaged theology or theology-engaged science. As Tolkien warns, "It's a dangerous business, Frodo, going out of your door"—"You step into the Road, and . . . there is no knowing where you might be swept off to."[8] And what we proposed in this little book is only part of the story, a way for an atheist scientist and an Orthodox theologian to experiment with science-engaged theology. Nevertheless, in the process of addressing cosmological issues from the viewpoint of our very different convictions and fields of expertise, we discovered something of relevance to trends in modern Orthodox theology. Thus, we found out that, when rigorous science is taken into consideration, such as the cosmological narrative of Chapter Two, Stăniloae's "theology of the world" and Nesteruk's universe of the self become the two sides of one coin—theology's New Copernican Turn—not two irreconcilable views of the universe. Consolidating the bridge between these views should count as yet another reason for pursuing a theological engagement of science.

Notes

1. See Matthew 22:21; Mark 12:17 (NRSV).
2. Henri Crouzel, *Origène*, Le Sycomore (Paris and Namur: Lethielleux and Culture et vérité, 1985), 84, 86, 222–23.
3. See Basil, *Homilies on the Hexaemeron* 2.3 and 3.7; Clement, *The Pedagogue* 1.1.1.1 and *Stromateis* 5.10.66; Evagrius Ponticus, *The Gnostic* (*Le Gnostique*) 4.1–4; Origen, *On First Principles* pref.1–3 etc.
4. McLeish, "The Rediscovery of Contemplation," 760.
5. See Costache, *Humankind and the Cosmos*, 1–2; Young, "Christian Teaching," 99.
6. Its oddness increases day by day. Take, for example, the very recent results of comparing the James Webb and Hubble Space Telescopes' measurements of cepheid stars, which confirm that the current cosmological models cannot explain the anisotropic expansion of the universe. See Adam G. Riess et al., "JWST Observations Reject Unrecognized Crowding of Cepheid Photometry as an Explanation for the Hubble Tension at 8σ Confidence," *The Astrophysical Journal Letters* 962:L17 (2024), DOI 10.3847/2041-8213/ad1ddd.
7. Tolkien, *The Lord of the Rings*, 84.
8. Tolkien, *The Lord of the Rings*, 74.

Bibliography

Premodern and Early Modern Sources

Adomnán of Iona: Vita Sancti Columbae. Edited by William Reeves. Dublin, 1857.
Athanase d'Alexandrie: Vie d'Antoine. Edited by G. J. M. Bartelink. Sources chrétiennes 400. Paris: Cerf, 1994.
Athanasius: Contra Gentes and De Incarnatione. Edited by Robert W. Thomson. Oxford Early Christian Texts. Oxford: Clarendon Press, 1971.
Athanasius: On Sickness and Health. In *Analecta patristica,* edited by F. Diekamp. Orientalia Christiana Analecta 117. Rome: Pontificium Institutum Orientalium Studiorum, 1962.
Augustine: Confessions, Vol. 1. Edited by James J. O'Donnell. Oxford: Clarendon Press, 1992.
Basile de Césarée: Homélies sur l'hexaéméron. Edited by Stanislas Giet. Sources chrétiennes 26. Paris: Cerf, 1949.
Bede: On Genesis. Translated by Calvin. B. Kendall. Translated Texts for Historians 48. Liverpool: Liverpool University Press, 2008.
Blaise Pascal: Opere Complete. Edited by Maria Vita Romeo. Il pensiero occidentale. Firenze: Bompiani, 2020.
Clemens Alexandrinus: Stromata Buch I—VI. Edited by Otto Stählin, Ludwig Früchtel, and Ursula Treu. Die griechischen christlichen Schriftsteller 15. Berlin: Akademie-Verlag, 1985.
Clément d'Alexandrie: Le Protreptique. Edited by Claude Mondésert. Sources chrétiennes 2. Paris: Cerf, 1949.
Die Schriften des Johannes von Damaskos, Vol. 2. Edited by P. B. Kotter. Patristische Texte und Studien 12. Berlin: De Gruyter, 1973.
Évagre le Pontique: Le Gnostique ou À celui qui est devenu digne de la science. Edited by Antoine Guillaumont et Claire Guillaumont. Sources chrétiennes 356. Paris: Cerf, 1989.
Évagre le Pontique: Sur les pensées. Edited by Paul Géhin, Claire Guillaumont, and Antoine Guillaumont. Sources chrétiennes 438. Paris: Cerf, 1998.
Évagre le Pontique: Traité pratique ou Le moine, Vol. 2. Edited by Antoine Guillaumont and Claire Guillaumont. Sources chrétiennes 171. Paris: Cerf, 1971.

108   Bibliography

Francis and Clare: The Complete Works. Translated by Regis J. Armstrong and Ignatius C. Brady. The Classics of Western Spirituality. New York: Paulist Press, 1982.

Grégoire de Nazianze: Discours 27–31 (Discours théologiques). Edited by Paul Gallay and Maurice Jourjon. Sources chrétiennes 250. Paris: Cerf, 1978.

Grégoire de Nazianze: Discours 38–41. Edited by Paul Gallay and Maurice Jourjon. Sources chrétiennes 358. Paris: Cerf, 1990.

Gregorii Nysseni In Hexaemeron: Opera Exegetica in Genesim, Part One. Edited by Hubertus R. Drobner. Leiden and Boston: Brill, 2009.

Gregory of Nyssa: On the Human Image of God. Edited by John Behr. Oxford Early Christian Texts. Oxford: Oxford University Press, 2023.

Maximi Confessoris Mystagogia, una cum latina interpretatione Anastasii Bibliothecarii. Edited by Christian Boudignon. Corpvs Christianorvm Series Graeca 69. Turnhout: Brepols, 2011.

Maximi Confessoris Quaestiones ad Thalassium, una cum interpretatione Ioannis Scotti Eriugenae iuxta posita, Vol. 2. Edited by Carl Laga and Carlos Steel. Corpvs Christianorvm Series Graeca 22. Turnhout: Brepols, 1990.

Maximos the Confessor: On Difficulties in the Church Fathers—The Ambigua, 2 Vols. Edited by Nicholas Constas. Dumbarton Oaks Medieval Library. Cambridge, MA and London: Harvard University Press, 2014.

New English Translation of the Septuagint and the Other Greek Translations Traditionally Included Under That Title (NETS). Edited by Albert Pietersma and Benjamin Wright. Oxford: Oxford University Press, 2007.

One Hundred Practical Texts of Perception and Spiritual Discernment From Diadochos of Photike. Edited by Janet Elaine Rutherford. Belfast Byzantine Texts and Translations 8. Belfast: Institute of Byzantine Studies and University of Belfast, 2000.

Origen: On First Principles. Edited by John Behr. Oxford Early Christian Texts. Oxford: Oxford University Press, 2017.

Popol Vuh: The Mayan Book of the Dawn of Life. Translated by Dennis Tedlock, revised ed. New York and London: Simon & Schuster, 1996.

Pseudo-Macarius. *Die 50 geistlichen Homilien des Makarios.* Edited by Hermann Dörries, Erich Klostermann, and Matthias Krüger. Patristische Texte und Studien 4. Berlin: De Gruyter, 1964.

René Descartes: Opere 1637–1649. Edited by Giulia Belgioioso. Il pensiero occidentale. Firenze: Bompiani, 2009.

Saint Gregory Palamas: The One Hundred and Fifty Chapters. Edited and Translated by Robert E. Sinkewicz. Studies and Texts 83. Toronto: Pontifical Institute of Mediaeval Studies, 1988.

Saint Gregory the Great: Dialogues. Translated by Odd John Zimmerman. The Fathers of the Church 39. Washington, DC: The Catholic University of America Press, 1959.

Sancti Basilii Homilia in Psalmum cxiv. Patrologiae cursus completus (series Graeca) 29, 484–93. Edited by Jacques-Paul Migne, 1857.

Sancti Johannis Chrysostomi Homiliae in Genesim. Patrologiae cursus completus (series Graeca) 53, 32–39. Edited by Jacques-Paul Migne, 1862.

The Sayings of the Desert Fathers: The Alphabetic Collection. Translated by Benedicta Ward. Cistercian Studies 59. Kalamazoo: Cistercian Publications, 1975.

Syméon le Nouveau Théologien: Traités théologiques et éthiques, Vol. 1. Edited by Jean Darrouzès. Sources chrétiennes 122. Paris: Cerf, 1966.

The Way of a Pilgrim and the Pilgrim Continues His Way. Translated by R. M. French. London: The Society for Promoting Christian Knowledge, 1996.

The Writings of Julian of Norwich: A Vision Showed to a Devout Woman and a Revelation of Love. Edited by Nicholas Watson and Jacqueline Jenkins. University Park, PA: The Pennsylvania State University Press, 2006.

Contemporary Sources

Adams, Douglas. *The Ultimate Hitchhiker's Guide to the Galaxy*. London: Pan Books, 2020.

Adams, Fred, and Greg Laughlin. *The Five Ages of the Universe: Inside the Physics of Eternity*. New York: Simon & Schuster, 2000.

Anatolios, Khaled. *Athanasius: The Coherence of His Thought*. London and New York: Routledge, 1998.

Aquino, Frederick D., and Paul L. Gavrilyuk (eds). *Perceiving Things Divine: Towards a Constructive Account of Spiritual Perception*. Oxford: Oxford University Press, 2022.

Ashwin-Siejkowski, Piotr. "Creeds, Councils, Doctrinal Development." In *The Early Christian World*, 2nd ed., edited by Philip F. Esler, 631–46. Routledge Worlds. London and New York: Routledge, 2017.

Bardi, Alberto. "The Archimedean Revolution of Nicolaus Copernicus." *Transversal: International Journal for the Historiography of Science* 14 (2023): 1–11. https://doi.org/10.24117/2526-2270.2022.i14.09.

Barnes, Luke A., and Geraint F. Lewis. *The Cosmic Revolutionary's Handbook (Or: How to Beat the Big Bang)*. Cambridge: Cambridge University Press, 2020.

Barrow, John D. *The Origin of the Universe*. Science Masters. New York: Basic Books, 1994.

———. *The Constants of Nature: From Alpha to Omega—The Numbers That Encode the Deepest Secrets of the Universe*. New York: Pantheon Books, 2002.

———. *New Theories of Everything: The Quest for Ultimate Explanation*. Oxford: Oxford University Press, 2007.

———, and Frank Tipler. *The Anthropic Cosmological Principle*. Oxford: Oxford University Press, 1988.

Batalias, Alexandros. "Emergentist Panentheism and Orthodox Theology: A Preliminary Encounter." *Theophany* 5 (2023): 45–77.

Beattie, Sarah Anne. "From Eden to Interstellar Space: Thomas Nagel, Biblical Hermeneutics and the Search for 'the True Extent of Reality'." PhD diss. Melbourne: University of Divinity, 2022.

Behr, John. "Introduction." In *Origen: On First Principles*, Vol. 1, edited by John Behr, xv–xcviii. Oxford Early Christian Texts. Oxford: Oxford University Press, 2017.

Betegh, Gábor. "Derveni papyrus (400–300 BCE?)." In *The Encyclopedia of Ancient Natural Scientists: The Greek Tradition and Its Many Heirs*, edited by Paul T. Keyser and Georgia L. Irby-Massie, 242–43. London and New York: Routledge, 2008.

Blaga, Lucian. "Eu nu strivesc corola de minuni a lumii." In *Poemele luminii (Poems of Light)*. Sibiu: Cosînzeana, 1919.

———. *Trilogia cunoașterii (Knowledge Trilogy)*. București: Humanitas, 2013.

Blowers, Paul M. *Drama of the Divine Economy: Creator and Creation in Early Christian Theology and Piety*. The Oxford Early Christian Studies. Oxford: Oxford University Press, 2012.

Bohm, David. *Wholeness and the Implicate Order*. London: Routledge, 1980.

———. "A New Theory of the Relationship of Mind and Matter." *Philosophical Psychology* 3, no. 2 (1990): 271–86. https://doi.org/10.1080/09515089008573004.

Bradshaw, David. "The *Logoi* of Beings in Greek Patristic Thought." In *Toward an Ecology of Transfiguration*, edited by John Chryssavgis and Bruce V. Foltz, 9–22. Orthodox Christianity and Contemporary Thought. New York: Fordham University Press, 2013.

———. "Introduction." In *Natural Theology in the Eastern Orthodox Tradition*, edited by David Bradshaw and Richard Swinburne, 1–21. St Paul, MN: IOTA Publications, 2021.

———, and Richard Swinburne (eds). *Natural Theology in the Eastern Orthodox Tradition*. St Paul, MN: IOTA Publications, 2021.

Brakke, David. *Athanasius and the Politics of Asceticism*. Oxford Early Christian Studies. Oxford: Clarendon Press, 1995.

———. *Demons and the Making of the Monk: Spiritual Combat in Early Christianity*. Cambridge, MA, and London, England: Harvard University Press, 2006.

Brisson, Luc. "Plato's Natural Philosophy and Metaphysics." In *A Companion to Ancient Philosophy*, edited by Mary Louise Gill and Pierre Pellegrin, 212–31. Blackwell Companions to Philosophy. Oxford: Blackwell Publishing, 2006.

Brown, Andrew J. *Recruiting the Ancients for the Creation Debate*. Grand Rapids, MI: Eerdmans, 2023.

Brown, Dan. *Origin*. London and Toronto: Bantam Press, 2017.

Capra, Fritjof. *The Tao of Physics: An Exploration of the Parallels Between Modern Physics ad Eastern Mysticism*. Boulder, CO: Shambala, 1975.

Casiday, Augustine. *Reconstructing the Theology of Evagrius Ponticus: Beyond Heresy*. Cambridge: Cambridge University Press, 2013.

Chapman, Emma. *First Light*. London: Bloomsbury, 2021.

Chryssavgis, John. *In the Heart of the Desert: The Spirituality of the Desert Fathers and Mothers*. Bloomington, IN: World Wisdom, 2003.

Ciobotea, Daniel. "O dogmatică pentru omul de azi" (Dogmatic Theology for Contemporary People). In *Dumitru Stăniloae sau Paradoxul Teologiei (Dumitru Staniloae or the Paradox of Theology)*, edited by Theodor Baconsky and Bogdan Tătaru-Cazaban, 87–107. București: Anastasia, 2003.

Clegg, Brian. *Dark Matter & Dark Energy: The Hidden 95% of the Universe*. Cheltenham: Icon, 2019.

Clottes, Jean. "The Paleolithic Cave Art of France." www.bradshawfoundation.com/clottes/index.php.

Clottes, Jean. *What Is Paleolithic Art: Cave Paintings and the Dawn of Human Creativity*. Translated by Oliver Y. Martin and Robert D. Martin. Chicago and London: University of Chicago Press, 2016.

Cooper, John M. *Pursuits of Wisdom: Six Ways of Life in Ancient Philosophy from Socrates to Plotinus*. Princeton and Oxford: Princeton University Press, 2012.

Costache, Doru. "Queen of the Sciences? Theology and Natural Knowledge in St Gregory Palamas' *One Hundred and Fifty Chapters*." *Transdisciplinarity in Science and Religion* 3 (2008): 27–46.

———. "Adam's Holiness in the Alexandrine and Athonite Traditions." In *Alexandrian Legacy: A Critical Appraisal*, edited by Doru Costache, Philip Kariatlis, and Mario Baghos, 322–68. Newcastle upon Tyne: Cambridge Scholars, 2015.

———. "Mapping Reality Within the Experience of Holiness." In *The Oxford Handbook of Maximus the Confessor*, edited by Pauline Allen and Bronwen Neil, 378–96. Oxford: Oxford University Press, 2015.

———. "John Moschus on Asceticism and the Environment." *Colloquium* 48, no. 1 (2016): 21–34.

———. "A Theology of the World: Dumitru Stăniloae, the Traditional Worldview, and Contemporary Cosmology." In *Orthodox Christianity and Modern Science: Tensions, Ambiguities, Potential*, edited by Vasilios N. Makrides and Gayle Woloschak, 205–22. Science and Orthodox Christianity 1. Turnhout: Brepols, 2019.

———. "Byzantine and Modern Orthodox Gnosis: From the Eleventh to the Twenty-First Century." In *The Gnostic World*, edited by Garry W. Trompf, Gunner B. Mikkelsen, and Jay Johnston, 426–35. Routledge Worlds. London and New York: Routledge, 2019.

———. "The Orthodox Doctrine of Creation in the Age of Science." *Journal of Orthodox Christian Studies* 2, no. 1 (2019c): 43–64.

———. "Maximus the Confessor and John Damascene's Cosmology." In *The T&T Clark Handbook of Christian Theology and the Modern Sciences*, edited by John Slattery, 81–91. London: Bloomsbury/T&T Clark, 2020.

———. "Strange Bedfellows? Orthodox Perspectives on Theology, Spirituality, Science, and Technology." *Studia Universitatis Babes-Bolyai Theologia Orthodoxa* 65, no. 2 (2020): 5–25.

———. "A Note on Evagrius' Cosmological and Metaphysical Statements." *The Journal of Theological Studies* 71, no. 2 (2020): 718–30.

———. *Humankind and the Cosmos: Early Christian Representations*. Supplements to Vigiliae Christianae 170. Leiden and Boston: Brill, 2021.

———. "One Description, Multiple Interpretations: Suggesting a Way Out of the Current Impasse." In *Orthodox Christianity and Modern Sciences: Theological, Philosophical, Scientific and Historical Aspects of the Dialogue*, edited by Christopher C. Knight and Alexei V. Nesteruk, 33–49. Science and Orthodox Christianity 2. Turnhout: Brepols, 2021.

———. "Affirming Creation's Goodness in a Time of Pandemic: Patristic Insights." *Colloquium* 54, no. 2 (2022): 9–32.

———. "Burning Hearts: Emmaus as Realised Eschatology in the *Philokalic* Tradition." In *God's Grace Inscribed on the Human Heart: Essays in Honour of James R. Harrison*, edited by Peter G. Bolt and Sehyun Kim, 61–78. Early Christian Studies 23. Macquarie Park: SCD Press, 2022.

———. "Theological Anthropology Today: Panayiotis Nellas's Contribution." In *Orthodox Christianity and Modern Science: Past, Present and Future*, edited by Kostas Tampakis and Haralampos Ventis, 167–82. Science and Orthodox Christianity 3. Turnhout: Brepols, 2022.

———. "Patristic and Neopatristic Antecedents of Scientifically Engaged Theology." *St Vladimir's Theological Quarterly* 67, nos. 1–2 (2023): 115–45.

———. "Abraham, the Contemplation of Nature, and Divine Vision in Clement of Alexandria." In *Knowing God in Light: Theophany and Language*, edited by Nichifor Tănase, Marius Portaru, and Daniel Lemeni. Berlin: LIT Verlag, forthcoming.

Crease, Robert P. "The Never-Ending Quest for a Beginning." *Nature* 616 (2023): 243–44. https://doi.org/10.1038/d41586-023-00977-3.

Crouzel, Henri. *Origène*. Le Sycomore. Paris and Namur: Lethielleux and Culture et vérité, 1985.

Danielson, Dennis. *Paradise Lost and the Cosmological Revolution*. Cambridge: Cambridge University Press, 2014.

Davies, Paul. *The Mind of God: Science and the Search for Ultimate Meaning*. London: Penguin Books, 1993.

———. *The Last Three Minutes*. New York: Basic Books, 1997.

Davison, Andrew (ed.). *Imaginative Apologetics: Theology, Philosophy and the Catholic Tradition*. London: SCM Press, 2011.

———. *Participation in God: A Study in Christian Doctrine and Metaphysics*. Cambridge: Cambridge University Press, 2019.

Davison, Andrew. "Science and Specificity: Interdisciplinary Teaching Between Theology, Religion, and the Natural Sciences." *Zygon* 57, no. 1 (2022): 233–43.

Dawkins, Richard. *The God Delusion*. London: Bantam Press, 2006.

Dempsey, Jack. "Cosmos Erotica: The Shapes of Minoan Desire." *jackdempseywriter* (28 January 2011). http://tinyurl.com/3tjpaxjt.

Dostoevsky, Fyodor. *The Brothers Karamazov*. Translated by Andrew R. MacAndrew. Bantam Classic. New York: Bantam Dell, 2003 (ebook ed.).

Douglas, Heather. "The Importance of Values for Science." *Interdisciplinary Science Reviews* 48, no. 2 (2023): 251–63. https://doi.org/10.1080/03080188.2023.2191559.

Duby, Georges. *L'An Mil*. Folio Histoire. Paris: Gallimard, 1980.

Edwards, Mark. "The Development of Office in the Early Church." In *The Early Christian World*, 2nd ed., edited by Philip F. Esler, 284–94. Routledge Worlds. London and New York: Routledge, 2017.

Einstein, Albert. "On the Method of Theoretical Physics." *Philosophy of Science* 1, no. 2 (1934): 163–69. https://doi.org/10.1086/286316.

Eire, Carlos M. N. *They Flew: A History of the Impossible*. New Haven, CT: Yale University Press, 2023.

Eklöf, Johan. *The Darkness Manifesto: On Light Pollution, Night Ecology, and the Ancient Rhythms That Sustain Life*. Translated by Elizabeth DeNoma. New York: Scribner, 2024.

Eliade, Mircea. *The Sacred and the Profane: The Nature of Religion*. Translated by Willard R. Trask. New York: Harcourt, 1959.

Ellis, George F. R. "A Foundational View of the Physics of Evolution." *Nature* 622 (2023): 247–49. https://doi.org/10.1038/d41586-023-03061-y.

Ferrie, Chris, and Geraint F. Lewis. *Where Did the Universe Come From? And Other Cosmic Questions: Our Universe, from the Quantum to the Cosmos*. Naperville, IL: Sourcebooks, 2021.

Flory, Mark W. "The Standpoint of Transformativity: Re-Envisioning Science, Nature, and the Self." In *Seeing and Being Seen: Aesthetics and Environmental Philosophy*, edited by Joshua Coleman, 58–68. Falls Village, CT: Hamilton Books, 2017.

Foltz, Bruce V. *Inhabiting the Earth: Heidegger, Environmental Ethics, and the Metaphysics of Nature*. Atlantic Highlands, NJ: Humanities Press, 1995.

———. "Traces of Divine Fragrance, Droplets of Divine Love: On the Beauty of Visible Creation." In *Toward an Ecology of Transfiguration*, edited by John Chryssavgis and Bruce V. Foltz, 324–36. Orthodox Christianity and Contemporary Thought. New York: Fordham University Press, 2013.

———. *The Noetics of Nature: Environmental Philosophy and the Holy Beauty of the Visible*. New York: Fordham University Press, 2014.

———. *Byzantine Incursions on the Borders of Philosophy: Contesting the Boundaries of Nature, Art, and Religion*. Cham: Springer, 2019.

———. "'The Lord Is in this Place, Yet I Did Not See It': From the Concept of Nature to the Experience of Creation." In *Orthodox Christianity and Modern Science: Theological, Philosophical, Scientific and Historical Aspects of the Dialogue*, edited by Christopher C. Knight and Alexei V. Nesteruk, 121–39. Science and Orthodox Christianity 2. Turnhout: Brepols, 2021.

Frank, Adam. "Science Claims a 'God's-Eye View' of Reality. This is Fiction." *Big Think*, June 8, 2023. http://tinyurl.com/5n6bksbv.

Freeland, Guy. "The Lamp in the Temple: Copernicus and the Demise of a Medieval Ecclesiastical Cosmology." In *1543 And All That: Image and Word, Change and Continuity in the Proto-Scientific Revolution*, edited by Guy Freeland and Anthony Corones, 189–270. Australasian Studies in History and Philosophy of Science 13. Dordrecht: Springer Science+Business Media, 2000.

Gavrilyuk, Paul L., and Sarah Coakley (eds). *The Spiritual Senses: Perceiving God in Western Christianity*. Cambridge: Cambridge University Press, 2012.

Gleede, Benjamin. "The Christian Rejection of Ptolemean Cosmography in (Late) Antiquity: Motives, Modalities, and Backgrounds." In *Platonism and Christianity in Late Ancient Cosmology: God, Soul, Matter*, edited by Ana Schiavoni-Palanciuc and Johannes Zachhuber, 184–204. Ancient Philosophy & Religion 9. Leiden and Boston: Brill, 2022.

Grant, Edward. *A History of Natural Philosophy: From the Ancient World to the Nineteenth Century*. Cambridge: Cambridge University Press, 2007.
Grey, Carmody. "A Theologian's Perspective on Science-Engaged Theology." *Modern Theology* 37, no. 2 (2021): 489–94.
Grijs, Richard de, and Doru Costache. "The Cosmology of David Bohm: Scientific and Theological Significance." *Theology and Science* 22, no. 1 (2023): 204–20. https://doi.org/10.1080/14746700.2023.2294529.
Hadot, Pierre. *Philosophy as a Way of Life: Spiritual Exercises from Socrates to Foucault*. Translated by Michael Chase. Oxford: Blackwell, 1995.
Hamacher, Duane. *The First Astronomers: How Indigenous Elders Read the Stars*. Sydney and Melbourne: Allen & Unwin, 2022.
Hanby, Michael. "Questioning the Science and Religion Question." In *After Science and Religion: Fresh Perspectives from Philosophy and Theology*, edited by Peter Harrison, John Milbank, and Paul Tyson, 155–70. Cambridge: Cambridge University Press, 2022.
Hankey, Wayne. "Natural Theology in the Patristic Period." In *The Oxford Handbook of Natural Theology*, edited by Russell Re Manning, 38–56. Oxford: Oxford University Press, 2013.
Harrison, Peter. *The Bible, Protestantism, and the Rise of Natural Science*. Cambridge: Cambridge University Press, 1998.
_____. *The Territories of Science and Religion*. Chicago and London: The University of Chicago Press, 2015.
_____. "Science, Eastern Orthodoxy, and Protestantism." *Isis* 107, no. 3 (2016): 587–91.
_____. "A Historian's Perspective on Science-Engaged Theology." *Modern Theology* 37, no. 2 (2021): 476–82.
Hart, David Bentley. *Atheist Delusions: The Christian Revolution and Its Fashionable Enemies*. New Haven and London: Yale University Press, 2009.
_____. "Science and Theology: Where the Consonance Really Lies." In *After Science and Religion: Fresh Perspectives from Philosophy and Theology*, edited by Peter Harrison, John Milbank, and Paul Tyson, 61–74. Cambridge: Cambridge University Press, 2022.
Havrda, Matyáš. "Demonstrative Method in *Stromateis* VII: Context, Principles, and Purpose." In *The Seventh Book of the Stromateis: Proceedings of the Colloquium on Clement of Alexandria*, edited by Matyáš Havrda, Vít Hušek, and Jana Plátová, 261–76. Supplements to Vigiliae Christianae 117. Leiden and Boston: Brill, 2012.
_____. *The So-Called Eighth* Stromateus *by Clement of Alexandria: Early Christian Reception of Greek Scientific Methodology*. Philosophia Antiqua 144. Leiden and Boston: Brill, 2017.
Hawking, Stephen. *Brief Answers to Big Questions*. London: John Murray, 2018.
Hawking, Steven. *A Brief History of Time*, updated and expanded 10th anniversary ed. New York: Bantam Books, 1996.
_____. *The Theory of Everything: The Origin and Fate of the Universe*, special anniversary ed. Beverly Hills, CA: Phoenix Books, 2005.

Hegedus, Tim. *Early Christianity and Ancient Astrology*. Patristic Studies 6. New York: Peter Lang, 2007.

Heine, Ronald E. "The Alexandrians." In *The Cambridge History of Early Christian Literature*, edited by Frances Young, Lewis Ayres, and Andrew Louth, 117–30. Cambridge: Cambridge University Press, 2004.

Heisenberg, Werner. *Physics and Philosophy: The Revolution in Modern Science*. World Perspectives. London: George Allen & Unwin, 1971.

Henry, Devin, and Karen Margarethe Nielsen. *Bridging the Gap Between Aristotle's Science and Ethics*. Cambridge: Cambridge University Press, 2015.

Hoggard Creegan, Nicola. "A Christian Theology of Evolution and Participation." *Zygon* 42, no. 2 (2007): 499–518.

Holland, Jocelyn, and Edgar Landgraf. "The Archimedean Point: From Fixed Positions to the Limits of Theory." *SubStance* 43, no. 3 (2014): 3–11.

Hooper, Dan. *At the Edge of Time: Exploring the Mysteries of Our Universe's First Seconds*. Princeton, NJ: Princeton University Press, 2020.

Hooper, Dan. *Dark Cosmos: In Search of Our Universe's Missing Mass and Energy*. New York: Harper Perennial, 2007.

Hossenfelder, Sabine. *Lost in Math: How Beauty Leads Physics Astray*. New York: Basic Books, 2018.

Howell, Christopher. "The Rose and the Stag: An American Orthodox Conversation on Modernity, Science, and Biblical Interpretation." *Almagest* 9, no. 2 (2019): 40–59.

———. "Between Darwin and Dostoevsky: The Syntheses of Theodosius Dobzhansky." *Christian Perspectives on Science and Technology, New Series* 1 (2022): 28–45.

Hutchinson, Keith. "The Natural, the Supernatural, and the Occult in the Scholastic Universe." In *1543 and All That: Image and Word, Change and Continuity in the Proto-Scientific Revolution*, edited by Guy Freeland and Anthony Corones, 333–55. Australasian Studies in History and Philosophy of Science 13. Dordrecht: Springer Science+Business Media, 2000.

Isaacson, Walter. *Einstein: His Life and Universe*. New York: Simon & Schuster, 2007.

Jeffrey, Richard C. "Valuation and Acceptance of Scientific Hypotheses." *Philosophy of Science* 23, no. 3 (1956): 237–46. https://doi.org/10.1086/287489.

Johnson, Diane. *Night Skies of Aboriginal Australia: A Noctuary*. Sydney: Sydney University Press, 2014.

Juurikkala, Oskari. "The Book of Nature in Patristic and Medieval Theology." *Interdisciplinary Documentation on Religion and Science 2003–2022* (2020). http://tinyurl.com/4prs2xsz.

Kaku, Michio. *Parallel Worlds: A Journey Through Creation, Higher Dimensions, and the Future of the Cosmos*. New York: Doubleday, 2006.

Katsos, Isidoros C. *The Metaphysics of Light in the Hexaemeral Literature: From Philo of Alexandria to Gregory of Nyssa*. Oxford: Oxford University Press, 2023.

Kazantzakis, Nikos. *Saint Francis*. Translated by P. A. Bien. Loyola Classics. Chicago: Loyola Press, 1962 (ebook ed.).

———. *Report to Greco*. Translated by P. A. Bien. New York: Simon and Schuster, 2012 (ebook ed.).
Kelley, David H., and Eugene F. Milone. *Exploring Ancient Skies: A Survey of Ancient and Cultural Astronomy*, 2nd ed. Astrophysics and Space Science Library 374. New York: Springer, 2011.
Knight, Christopher C. *The God of Nature: Incarnation and Contemporary Science*. Theology and the Sciences. Minneapolis, MN: Augsburg Fortress Publishers, 2007.
———. "Natural Theology and the Eastern Orthodox Tradition." In *The Oxford Handbook of Natural Theology*, edited by Russell Re Manning, 213–26. Oxford: Oxford University Press, 2013.
———. "Divine Action and the Laws of Nature: An Orthodox Perspective on Miracles." In *Science and the Eastern Orthodox Church*, edited by Daniel Buxhoeveden and Gayle Woloschak, 41–51. London and New York: Routledge, 2016.
———. *Science and the Christian Faith: A Guide for the Perplexed. Foundations*. Crestwood, NY: St Vladimir's Seminary Press, 2021.
———. *Eastern Orthodoxy and the Science-Theology Dialogue*. Cambridge Elements: Elements of Christianity and Science. Cambridge: Cambridge University Press, 2022.
———, and Alexei V. Nesteruk (eds). *Orthodox Christianity and Modern Science: Theological, Philosophical, Scientific and Historical Aspects of the Dialogue*. Science and Orthodox Christianity 2. Turnhout: Brepols, 2021.
Köckert, Charlotte. *Christliche Kosmologie und kaiserzeitliche Philosophie: Die Auslegung des Schöpfungsberichtes bei Origenes, Basilius und Gregor von Nyssa vor dem Hintergrund kaiserzeitlicher Timaeus-Interpretationen*. Studien und Texte zu Antike und Christentum 56. Tübingen: Mohr Siebeck, 2009.
Koertge, Loretta. "Philosophy of the Social Sciences." In *The Philosophy of Science: An Encyclopedia*, edited by Sahotra Sarkar and Jessica Pfeifer, 780–85. New York and London: Routledge, 2006.
Koestler, Arthur. *The Sleepwalkers: A History of Man's Changing Vision of the Universe*. New York: Macmillan, 1959.
Koyré, Alexandre. *From the Closed World to the Infinite Universe*. Baltimore, MD: The Johns Hopkins Press, 1957.
Kragh, Helge. "Hubble Law or Hubble-Lemaître Law? The IAU Resolution." arXiv, September 7, 2018. https://arxiv.org/abs/1809.02557.
———. "How the Big Bang Got Its Name." *Nature* 627 (2024): 726–28. https://doi.org/10.1038/d41586-024-00894-z.
Krauss, Lawrence. *A Universe from Nothing: Why Is There Something Rather Than Nothing*. New York: Atria, 2013.
La Matina, Marcello. "On Subjects, Objects, Transitional Fields, and Icons: The Semiotics of a New Paradigm in Human Studies." *Christian Perspectives on Science and Technology*, New Series, 1 (2022): 108–49.
———. "The State of Things to Come: The Notion of Truth between Contemporary Philosophy of Language and Fourth-Century Eastern Patristics." *Blityri* 11, nos. 1–2 (2022): 97–118.
Lazaris, Stavros (ed.). *A Companion to Byzantine Science*. Brill Companions to the Byzantine World 6. Leiden and Boston: Brill, 2020.

Leidenhag, Joanna. *Minding Creation: Theological Panpsychism and the Doctrine of Creation*. T&T Clark Studies in Systematic Theology 37. London: T&T Clark, 2021.
Lemeni, Adrian. "References of Father Dumitru Stăniloae's Thought in the Dialogue Between Theology and Science." In *Orthodox Christianity and Modern Science: Theological, Philosophical, Scientific and Historical Aspects of the Dialogue*, edited by Christopher C. Knight and Alexei V. Nesteruk, 155–63. Science and Orthodox Christianity 2. Turnhout: Brepols, 2021.
Lewis, C. S. *The Space Trilogy: Out of the Silent Planet—Perelandra—That Hideous Strength*. London: Harper Collins Publishers, 2013.
Lewis, Geraint F., and Luke A. Barnes. *A Fortunate Universe: Life in a Finely Tuned Cosmos*. Cambridge: Cambridge University Press, 2016.
Lightman, Alan, and Roberta Brower. *Origins: The Lives and Worlds of Modern Cosmologists*. Cambridge, MA: Harvard University Press, 1990.
Lindberg, David C. *The Beginnings of Western Science: The European Scientific Tradition in Philosophical, Religious, and Institutional Context, Prehistory to A.D. 1450*, 2nd ed. Chicago and London: The University of Chicago Press, 2007.
———. "The Fate of Science in Patristic and Medieval Christendom." In *The Cambridge Companion to Science and Religion*, edited by Peter Harrison, 21–38. Cambridge: Cambridge University Press, 2010.
Lollar, Joshua. *To See into the Life of Things: The Contemplation of Nature in Maximus the Confessor and His Predecessors*. Monothéisme et philosophie. Turnhout: Brepols, 2013.
Lombriser, Lucas. "Cosmology in Minkowski Space." *Classical and Quantum Gravity* 40, no. 15 (2023): 155005. https://doi.org/10.1088/1361-6382/acdb41.
Longair, Malcolm. *The Cosmic Century*. Cambridge: Cambridge University Press, 2013.
Lossky, Vladimir. *The Mystical Theology of the Eastern Church*. Crestwood, NY: St Vladimir's Seminary Press, 2002.
Lössl, Josef. "Tatian, Theophilus of Antioch and Irenaeus of Lyons." In *The Routledge Handbook of Early Christian Philosophy*, edited by Mark Edwards, 342–56. London and New York: Routledge, 2021.
Louth, Andrew. "Basil and the Greek Fathers on Creation in the *Hexaemeron*." In *The T&T Clark Handbook of Christian Theology and the Modern Sciences*, edited by John Slattery, 67–79. London: Bloomsbury/T&T Clark, 2020.
Louth, Andrew. *Discerning the Mystery: An Essay on the Nature of Theology*. Oxford: Clarendon Press, 1989.
———. "The Theology of the *Philokalia*." In *Abba: The Tradition of Orthodoxy in the West*, edited by John Behr, Andrew Louth, and Dimitri Conomos, 351–61. Crestwood, NY: St Vladimir's Seminary Press, 2003.
———. "The Six Days of Creation According to the Greek Fathers." In *Reading Genesis After Darwin*, edited by Stephen C. Barton and David Wilkinson, 39–55. New York: Oxford University Press, 2009.
———. *Introducing Eastern Orthodox Theology*. Downers Grove, IL: IVP Academic, 2013.

_____. "Man and Cosmos in St. Maximus the Confessor." In *Toward an Ecology of Transfiguration*, edited by John Chryssavgis and Bruce V. Foltz, 59–71. Orthodox Christianity and Contemporary Thought. New York: Fordham University Press, 2013.

_____. *Modern Orthodox Thinkers: From the Philokalia to the Present*. London: Society for Promoting Christian Knowledge, 2015.

Lovecraft, H. P. "Supernatural Horror in Literature." In *The Fiction: Complete and Unabridged*. New York: Barnes & Noble, 2008.

Mack, Katie. *The End of Everything (Astrophysically Speaking)*. London: Allen Lane, 2020.

MacKinnell, Terry. *The Dawning: Shedding New Light on the Astrological Ages*. Bloomington, IN: Xlibris, 2011.

Makrides, Vasilios N. "The Natural Sciences in the Framework of a European History of Religion." In *Religion in Culture—Culture in Religion*, edited by Christoph Auffarth, Alexandra Grieser, and Anne Koch, 271–94. Tübingen: Tübingen University Press, 2021.

_____. "Orthodoxy Matters: Why Has a Scientific Revolution Not Taken Place in the Greek East?" In *Orthodox Christianity and Modern Science: Past, Present and Future*, edited by Kostas Tampakis and Haralampos Ventis, 15–44. Science and Orthodox Christianity 3. Turnhout: Brepols, 2022.

_____, and Gayle Woloschak (eds). *Orthodox Christianity and Modern Science: Tensions, Ambiguities, Potential*. Science and Orthodox Christianity 1. Turnhout: Brepols, 2019.

McGrath, Alister E., and Joanna Collicutt McGrath. *The Dawkins Delusion: Atheist Fundamentalism and the Denial of the Divine*. Downers Grove, IL: IVP Books, 2007.

McGuckin, John Anthony. "The Making of the *Philokalia*: A Tale of Monks and Manuscripts." In *The Philokalia: A Classic Text of Orthodox Spirituality*, edited by Brock Bingaman and Bradley Nassif, 36–49. New York: Oxford University Press, 2012.

_____. "The Beauty of the World and Its Significance in St. Gregory the Theologian." In *Toward an Ecology of Transfiguration*, edited by John Chryssavgis and Bruce V. Foltz, 34–45. Orthodox Christianity and Contemporary Thought. New York: Fordham University Press, 2013.

McLeish, Tom. *Faith and Wisdom in Science*. Oxford: Oxford University Press, 2014.

_____. *The Poetry and Music of Science: Comparing Creativity in Science and Art*. Oxford: Oxford University Press, 2019.

_____. "Before Science and Religion: Learning from Medieval Physics." *Modern Believing* 62, no. 2 (2021): 124–35. https://doi.org/10.3828/mb.2021.9.

_____. "The Rediscovery of Contemplation Through Science." *Zygon* 56, no. 3 (2021): 758–76. https://doi.org/10.1111/zygo.12719.

Meijering, E. P. *Orthodoxy and Platonism in Athanasius: Synthesis or Antithesis?* Reprint With Corrections. Leiden: Brill, 1974.

Meixner, Uwe. "Orthodox Panentheism: Sergius Bulgakov's Sophiology." In *Panentheism and Panpsychism: Philosophy of Religion Meets Philosophy of Mind*, edited by Godehard Brüntrup, Benedikt Paul Göcke, and Ludwig

Jaskolla, 205–30. Innsbruck Studies in Philosophy of Religion 2. Leiden and Boston: Brill and mentis, 2020.
Mellas, Andrew. "The Chora Within: Unveiling Asceticism in St Athanasius' *Life of St Antony*." In *Alexandrian Legacy: A Critical Appraisal*, edited by Doru Costache, Philip Kariatlis, and Mario Baghos, 122–38. Newcastle upon Tyne: Cambridge Scholars, 2015.
Mendell, Henry. "Aristarkhos of Samos (ca 280–270 BCE)." In *The Encyclopedia of Ancient Natural Scientists: The Greek Tradition and Its Many Heirs*, edited by Paul T. Keyser and Georgia L. Irby-Massie, 131–33. London and New York: Routledge, 2008.
Meyendorff, John. *Byzantine Theology: Historical Trends and Doctrinal Themes*. New York: Fordham University Press, 1979.
Minami, Yuto, and Eiichiro Komatsu. "A Hint of New Physics in Polarized Radiation from the Early Universe." Max Planck Institute for Astrophysics (November 2020). https://tinyurl.com/ycyat6tj.
Mironescu, Alexandru. *Certitudine și adevăr (Certainty and Truth)*. București: Harisma, 1992.
Nagel, Thomas. *Mind and Cosmos: Why the Materialist Neo-Darwinian Conception of Nature Is Almost Certainly False*. New York: Oxford University Press, 2012.
Neil, Bronwen, Doru Costache, and Kevin Wagner. *Dreams, Virtue and Divine Knowledge in Early Christian Egypt*. Cambridge: Cambridge University Press, 2019.
Nellas, Panayiotis. *Deification in Christ: Orthodox Perspectives on the Nature of the Human Person*. Translated by Norman Russell. Contemporary Greek Theologians 5. Crestwood, NY: St Vladimir's Seminary Press, 1997.
Nesteruk, Alexei V. *Light from the East: Theology, Science, and the Orthodox Christian Tradition*. Theology and the Sciences. Minneapolis: Fortress Press, 2003.
_____. *The Universe as Communion: Towards a Neo-Patristic Synthesis of Theology and Science*. London: T&T Clark, 2008.
_____. *The Sense of the Universe: Philosophical Explication of Theological Commitment in Modern Cosmology*. Minneapolis: Fortress Press, 2015.
_____. "Humanity as the Central Theme of the Dialogue Between Theology and Science." In *Orthodox Christianity and Modern Science: Past, Present and Future*, edited by Kostas Tampakis and Haralampos Ventis, 147–66. Science and Orthodox Christianity 3. Turnhout: Brepols, 2022.
_____. *The Universe in the Image of Imago Dei: The Dialogue Between Theology and Science as a Hermeneutics of the Human Condition*. Eugene, OR: Pickwick, 2022.
Newman, Cardinal John Henry. *On the Scope and Nature of University Education*. Everyman's Library 723. London and New York: Dent and Dutton, 1965.
Nicholas, Frank W. "Religion's Openness Towards Science." *Nature* 546 (2017): 474.
Nicolaidis, Efthymios. *Science and Eastern Orthodoxy: From the Greek Fathers to the Age of Globalization*. Translated by Susan Emanuel. Baltimore: The Johns Hopkins University Press, 2011.

———. "Creationism in Today's Orthodox Community." *Almagest* 12 (2021): 208–27. https://doi.org/10.1484/J.ALMAGEST.5.125391.

———, Eudoxie Delli, Nikolaos Livanos, Kostas Tampakis, and George Vlahakis. "Science and Orthodox Christianity: An Overview." *Isis* 107, no. 3 (2011): 542–66.

Nicolescu, Basarab. *Nous, la particule et le monde*, 2nd ed. Monaco: Éditions du Rocher, 2002.

———. *From Modernity to Cosmodernity: Science, Culture, and Spirituality.* SUNY Series in Western Esoteric Traditions. Albany, NY: State University of New York Press, 2014.

Norris, Richard A. "Articulating Identity." In *The Cambridge History of Early Christian Literature*, edited by Frances Young, Lewis Ayres, and Andrew Louth, 71–90. Cambridge: Cambridge University Press, 2004.

———. "Irenaeus of Lyon." In *The Cambridge History of Early Christian Literature*, edited by Frances Young, Lewis Ayres, and Andrew Louth, 45–52. Cambridge: Cambridge University Press, 2004.

———. "The Apostolic and Sub-Apostolic Writings: The New Testament and the Apostolic Fathers." In *The Cambridge History of Early Christian Literature*, edited by Frances Young, Lewis Ayres, and Andrew Louth, 11–19. Cambridge: Cambridge University Press, 2004.

Nowak, Martin A., and Sarah Coakley (eds). *Evolution, Games, and God: The Principle of Cooperation.* Cambridge, MA and London, England: Harvard University Press, 2013.

O'Brien, Glen. "'Creatures Capable of God': John Wesley's Theological Anthropology and the Posthuman Future." In *A Curious Machine: Wesleyan Reflections on the Posthuman Future*, edited by Arseny Ermakov and Glen O'Brien, 13–32. Eugene, OR: Wipf and Stock, 2023.

O'Callaghan, Jonathan. "A Background 'Hum' Pervades the Universe. Scientists Are Racing to Find Its Source." *Scientific American*, August 4, 2023. http://tinyurl.com/mpm5f2py.

Pais, Abraham. *Subtle is the Lord: The Science and Life of Albert Einstein.* Oxford: Oxford University Press, 2005.

Paulson, Steve, Lisa Sideris, Jennifer Stellar, and Piercarlo Valdesolo. "Beyond Oneself: The Ethics and Psychology of Awe." *Annals of the New York Academy of Sciences* 1501, no. 1, Special Issue: *The Power of Wonder: Modern Marvels in the Age of Science* (2021): 30–47. https://doi.org/10.1111/nyas.14323.

Peeble, Jim. *Cosmology's Century.* Princeton, NJ: Princeton University Press, 2020.

Penrose, Roger. *The Emperor's New Mind: Concerning Computers, Minds, and the Laws of Physics.* New York: Penguin Books, 1991.

———. *The Road to Reality: A Complete Guide to the Laws of the Universe.* London: Jonathan Cape, 2004.

———, and Stuart Hameroff (eds). *Consciousness and the Universe: Quantum Physics, Evolution, Brain & Mind.* Cambridge, MA: Cosmology Science Publishers, 2011.

Percy, Walker. *Lost in the Cosmos: The Last Self-Help Book.* New York: Open Road, 2011 (ebook ed.; 1st ed., 1983).

Perry, John, and Joanna Leidenhag. "What Is Science-Engaged Theology?" *Modern Theology* 37, no. 2 (2021): 245–53.
———. *Science-Engaged Theology*. Cambridge Elements: Elements of Christianity and Science. Cambridge: Cambridge University Press, 2023.
Popper, Karl. *In Search of a Better World: Lectures and Essays from Thirty Years*. Translated by Laura J. Bennett. London and New York: Routledge, 1994.
———. *Knowledge and the Mind-Body Problem: In Defence of Interaction*. London and New York: Routledge, 1994.
Pratt Morris-Chapman, Daniel. "Beyond the Quadrilateral: The Place of Nature in John Wesley's Epistemology of Theology." *HTS Teologiese Studies/Theological Studies* 78, no. 2 (2022): 1–8. https://doi.org/10.4102/hts.v78i2.7643.
Preston, Jesse L., Thomas J. Coleman III, and Faith Shin. "Spirituality of Science: Implications for Meaning, Well-Being, and Learning." *Personality and Social Psychology Bulletin* (2023). https://doi.org/10.1177/01461672231191356.
Radder, Hans. "Experiment." In *The Philosophy of Science: An Encyclopedia*, edited by Sahotra Sarkar and Jessica Pfeifer, 268–75. New York and London: Routledge, 2006.
Remes, Pauliina, and Juha Sihvola (eds). *Ancient Philosophy of the Self*. The New Synthese Historical Library 64. Dordrecht: Springer, 2008.
Riess, Adam G., Gagandeep S. Anand, Wenlong Yuan, Stefano Casertano, Andrew Dolphin, Lucas M. Macri, Louise Breuval, Dan Scolnic, Marshall Perrin, and Richard I. Anderson. "JWST Observations Reject Unrecognized Crowding of Cepheid Photometry as an Explanation for the Hubble Tension at 8σ Confidence." *The Astrophysical Journal Letters* 962 (2024): L17. https://doi.org/10.3847/2041-8213/ad1ddd.
Rizzerio, Laura. *Clemente di Alessandria e la "φυσιολογία veramente gnostica": Saggio sulle origini e le implicazioni di un'epistemologia e di un'ontologia 'cristiane.'* Leuven: Peeters, 1996.
Rudner, Richard. "The Scientist *Qua* Scientist Makes Value Judgments." *Philosophy of Science* 20, no. 1 (1953): 1–6. https://doi.org/10.1086/287231.
Ruggles, Clive. *Ancient Astronomy: An Encyclopedia of Cosmologies and Myth*. Santa Barbara, CA: ABC Clio, 2005.
Rumsfeld, Secretary of Defense Donald H. "DoD News Briefing." U. S. Department of Defense, February 12, 2002. http://tinyurl.com/4apf6zb6.
Sagan, Carl. *Contact*. New York: Gallery Books, 2019.
Scheck, Thomas P. "Origen." In *The Early Christian World*, 2nd ed., edited by Philip F. Esler, 943–58. Routledge Worlds. London and New York: Routledge, 2017.
Sharma, Abhishek, Dániel Czégel, Michael Lachmann, Christopher P. Kempes, Sara I. Walker, and Leroy Cronin. "Assembly Theory Explains and Quantifies Selection and Evolution." *Nature* 622 (2023): 321–29. https://doi.org/10.1038/s41586-023-06600-9.
Shatner, William. "My Trip to Space Made Me Realise We Have Only One Earth—It Must Live Long and Prosper." *The Guardian*, December 7, 2022. https://tinyurl.com/53x45fz5.

Bibliography

Sideris, Lisa H. *Consecrating Science: Wonder, Knowledge, and the Natural World*. Berkeley, CA: University of California Press, 2017.

———. "Wonder Sustained: A Reply to Critics." *Zygon* 54, no. 2 (2019): 1–28.

———. "Is Wonder at the Scientific Enterprise Good for Us, and for Our Relationship to the Natural World?" *Annals of the New York Academy of Sciences* 1501, no. 1, special issue: *The Power of Wonder: Modern Marvels in the Age of Science* (2021): 67–74. https://doi.org/10.1111/nyas.14490.

———. "To Benefit from Wonder, Make Sure You've Got the Genuine Kind." *Psyche*, October 4, 2022. https://tinyurl.com/yj4efddj.

———. "Religion." In *Handbook of the Anthropocene: Humans Between Heritage and Future*, edited by Nathanaël Wallenhorst and Christoph Wulf, 905–10. Cham: Springer, 2024. https://doi.org/10.1007/978-3-031-25910-4_148.

Smith, Brent. *Religious Studies and the Goal of Interdisciplinarity*. Routledge Focus. London and New York: Routledge, 2020.

Smolin, Lee. *Life of the Cosmos*. Oxford: Oxford University Press, 1997.

———. *The Trouble With Physics: The Rise of String Theory, the Fall of Science, and What Comes Next*. London: Penguin, 2008.

Somerville, Margaret. *The Ethical Imagination: Journeys of the Human Spirit*. The Massey Lectures. Toronto, ON: Anansi, 2006 (ebook ed.).

———. "Could 'The Wonder Equation' Help Us To Be More Ethical? A Personal Reflection." *Ethics & Behavior* 32, no. 3 (2022): 226–40. https://doi.org/10.1080/10508422.2020.1867861.

Stapp, Henry P. *Mindful Universe: Quantum Mechanics and the Participating Observer*, 2nd ed. Berlin and Heidelberg: Springer, 2011.

Stăniloae, Dumitru. *Theology and the Church*. Translated by Robert Barringer. Crestwood, NY: St Vladimir's Seminary Press, 1980.

———. "Introducere." In *Sfântul Atanasie cel Mare: Scrieri*, first part, edited by Dumitru Stăniloae, 5–26. Părinţi şi Scriitori Bisericeşti 15. Bucureşti: Editura Institutului Biblic şi de Misiune al Bisericii Ortodoxe Române, 1987.

———. *Iisus Hristos, lumina lumii şi îndumnezeitorul omului (Jesus Christ, Light of the World and Deifier of Humankind)*. Bucureşti: Anastasia, 1993.

———. *Teologia dogmatică ortodoxă (Orthodox Dogmatic Theology)*, 3 Vols, 3rd ed. Bucureşti: Editura Institutului Biblic şi de Misiune al Bisericii Ortodoxe Române, 2003 (1st ed., 1979).Steinhardt, Paul, and Neil Turok. *Endless Universe: Beyond the Big Bang*. New York: Doubleday, 2007.

Stellar, Jennifer E. "Awe Helps Us Remember Why It Is Important to Forget the Self." *Annals of the New York Academy of Sciences* 1501, no. 1, special issue: *The Power of Wonder: Modern Marvels in the Age of Science* (2021): 81–84. https://doi.org/10.1111/nyas.14577.

Tampakis, Kostas, and Haralampos Ventis (eds). *Orthodox Christianity and Modern Science: Past, Present and Future*. Science and Orthodox Christianity 3. Turnhout: Brepols, 2022.

Tanev, Stoyan. *Energy in Orthodox Theology and Physics: From Controversy to Encounter*. Eugene, OR: Pickwick, 2017.

Teilhard de Chardin, Pierre. *Le phénomène humain*. Paris: Seuil, 1956.

———. *Le Milieu Divin: An Essay on the Interior Life*. London: Collins, 1962.
Theokritoff, Elizabeth. "Creator and Creation." In *The Cambridge Companion to Orthodox Christian Theology*, edited by Mary B. Cunningham and Elizabeth Theokritoff, 63–77. Cambridge: Cambridge University Press, 2008.
———, and Christopher C. Knight. "Twentieth- and Twenty-First-Century Orthodox Voices on Nature and Science." In *The T&T Clark Handbook of Christian Theology and the Modern Sciences*, edited by John Slattery, 177–90. London: Bloomsbury/T&T Clark, 2020.
Tihon, Anne. "Alexandrian Astronomy in the 2nd Century Ad: Ptolemy and His Times." In *The Alexandrian Tradition: Interactions Between Science, Religion, and Literature*, edited by Luis Arturo Guichard, Juan Luis García Alonso, and María Paz de Hoz, 73–91. Ricerche di cultura europea 28. Bern and Berlin: Peter Lang, 2014.
Tolkien, J. R. R. *The Lord of the Rings*, 15th anniversary ed. New York: HarperCollins, 2004.
Tyson, Paul. "Introduction: After Science and Religion?" In *After Science and Religion: Fresh Perspectives from Philosophy and Theology*, edited by Peter Harrison, John Milbank, and Paul Tyson, 1–11. Cambridge: Cambridge University Press, 2022.
———. "Learned Ignorance? On Enlightened Blindness to the Divine and the Demonic." *Christian Perspectives on Science and Technology*, New Series, 3 (2024): 1–26. https://doi.org/10.58913/YWEV1287.
Vonnegut, Kurt. *The Sirens of Titan*. New York: Rosetta Books, 2000 (ebook ed.; 1st ed., 1959).
Wagner, Roger, and Andrew Briggs. *The Penultimate Curiosity: How Science Swims in the Slipstream of Ultimate Questions*. Oxford: Oxford University Press, 2016.
Wallace-Hadrill, D. S. *The Greek Patristic View of Nature*. Manchester and New York: Manchester University Press and Barns & Noble, 1968.
Ware, Kallistos. "God Immanent Yet Transcendent: The Divine Energies According to Saint Gregory Palamas." In *In Whom We Live and Move and Have Our Being: Panentheistic Reflections on God's Presence in a Scientific World*, edited by Philip Clayton and Arthur Robert Peacocke, 157–68. Grand Rapids, MI and Cambridge: Eerdmans, 2004.
Weinberg, Steven. *The First Three Minutes: A Modern View of the Origin of the Universe*, updated ed. New York: Basic Books, 1993.
Woit, Peter. *Not Even Wrong: The Failure of String Theory and the Continuing Challenge to Unify the Laws of Physics*. London: Vintage, 2011.
Yannaras, Christos. *Elements of Faith: An Introduction to Orthodox Theology*. Translated by Keith Schram. Edinburgh: T&T Clark, 1991.
Young, Frances. "Christian Teaching." In *The Cambridge History of Early Christian Literature*, edited by Frances Young, Lewis Ayres, and Andrew Louth, 91–104. Cambridge: Cambridge University Press, 2004.

Index of Names

Adams, Douglas 69, 74, 94n14, 96n52
Adomnán of Iona 55, 65n134, 99n118
Antony of Egypt 83, 86–8
Athanasius of Alexandria 47, 71, 82–4, 86–8, 90
Augustine of Hippo 37, 39, 71, 92

Basil of Caesarea 3, 4, 41, 44–7, 52, 53, 55
Bede the Venerable 46
Blaga, Lucian 77, 81
Blowers, Paul 59n19, 62n74, 86
Bohm, David 50, 53, 63n103, 78, 79, 89

Capra, Fritjof 50, 53
Clement of Alexandria 4, 7, 9, 37, 39, 41, 48, 55, 79, 82, 84–6, 88, 90, 92
Columba 85, 90

Davison, Andrew 7, 42
Descartes, René 38, 71, 73, 78, 88, 94, 105
Diadochus of Photiki 55
Dostoevsky, Fyodor 88–91

Einstein, Albert 21, 22, 25, 28, 29, 77
Evagrius Ponticus 83, 86, 95n25, 99n120

Foltz, Bruce 73, 89, 92, 93
Francis of Assisi 80, 81, 87, 98n103
Friedmann, Alexander 21, 22

Gregory of Nyssa 3, 4, 47, 52, 53, 79
Gregory Palamas 48, 62n86
Gregory the Great 55
Gregory the Theologian 55, 78
Grey, Carmody 7, 16n35

Hossenfelder, Sabine 34n13, 69, 75
Hubble, Edwin 21, 22

John Chrysostom 37, 52, 55
John Damascene 4, 46
Julian of Norwich 55

Kazantzakis, Nikos 80, 81, 82, 86–9
Kelvin, William Thomson 26
Knight, Christopher 2, 47, 54, 60n40

La Matina, Marcello 49, 56n1, 79
Leidenhag, Joanna 7, 63n102
Lemaitre, Georges 22, 27
Lewis, C. S. 39
Lossky, Vladimir 4–6, 37, 42–4, 55, 81
Louth, Andrew 14n20, 43, 78
Lovecraft, H. P. 74

Makrides, Vasilios N. 39, 59n31
Maximus the Confessor 43, 46, 55, 78

McLeish, Tom 72, 79, 84, 91, 92, 103
Meyendorff, John 41, 42, 52

Nagel, Thomas 50
Nellas, Panayiotis 4, 5, 43
Nesteruk, Alexei 9, 12, 38, 43, 47, 49, 70, 78, 106
Newman, John Henry 7, 37, 43
Newton, Isaac 21, 36, 37
Nicholas, Frank W. 41, 52
Nicolescu, Basarab 50, 72, 73, 86, 92

Pascal, Blaise 39, 68–71, 73, 75, 77, 78, 88, 104, 105
Penrose, Roger 49, 74, 79
Percy, Walker 67–70, 72–5, 77–9, 86, 92, 93, 104
Perry, John 7, 13n7
(Abba) Poemen 75
Popper, Karl 72, 92
Pseudo-Macarius 82

Rizzerio, Laura 84, 100n135
Rubin, Vera 25
Russian Pilgrim 87, 88, 90, 91

Sagan, Carl 78
Sideris, Lisa H. 7, 50, 90, 91, 101n160
Somerville, Margaret 72, 77, 79, 86
Stăniloae, Dumitru 4, 5, 8, 9, 12, 43, 47, 54, 55, 73, 81, 106
Stapp, Henry 79, 98n93
Symeon the New Theologian 46

Teilhard de Chardin, Pierre 37, 45, 48–50, 54, 55, 68, 72, 74, 78, 79, 93, 97n79, 102n184
Tolkien, J. R. R. 12, 82, 106
Tyson, Paul 13n2, 18n55, 37

Vonnegut, Kurt 68, 69, 77, 82

Weinberg, Steven 33n6, 68, 69, 71, 89, 90

Yannaras, Christos 37

Thematic Index

anthropic principle 8, 31, 73, 78, 96n50
anthropocentrism 38, 39, 75, 89, 93
anxiety 12, 88, 105
apologists 2, 41–4, 51, 54
apophaticism 37, 44, 49, 57n9, 77, 105
Archimedean point 71, 95n29

Big Bang 22, 23, 27, 28, 30–2, 47
Big Crunch 31

complexity (of nature) 6, 10, 21, 27, 30, 43, 47, 56, 78, 80, 81, 83, 86, 90, 93
complex thinking 4, 5, 11, 12, 71–3
comprehensive worldview 37, 42, 44, 49, 77, 88, 91–3
constants of nature 29
contemplation of nature 1, 7, 10, 12, 38, 47, 54, 56, 67, 79, 80–4, 86–93
cooperation *see* synergy
Cretan Glance 80, 86

dark side 11, 25–6, 28–9, 30, 31, 32, 39, 44, 48–9, 53, 73, 74
divine activity 3, 10, 35, 38, 39, 41, 45–7, 51–4, 55, 56, 83

exile *see* predicament of the self
existential dimension 38, 39, 67–9, 72, 73, 78, 84, 85, 92, 103
expansion of the universe 6, 8, 22–3, 25–6, 27–32, 43, 44, 76, 106n6

fine-tuning 30–1, 34n15, 81, 87

geocentric model *see* Ptolemaic system
gravity 11, 19, 21, 23–5, 28, 29

heliocentric model 3, 12n1, 67, 94n1

infinite universe 19, 28, 38, 39, 67–9, 75, 88, 89, 104, 105
introspection 70, 82, 83

knowns and unknowns 1, 2, 7, 8, 10–11, 27, 37, 38, 76, 79, 93, 103, 104

Lectio divina 86

methodological naturalism *see* scientific method
mortality (of the universe) 32, 47, 83, 104
multiverse 28, 31, 33, 39, 44, 56, 68, 70, 73

natural (aspect of reality) 4, 5, 8, 10, 41, 47, 48, 50–6, 67, 74, 82–4, 93, 104, 106
neopatristic thinking 4–8
New Copernican Turn 1, 3, 10, 12, 38, 54, 67, 68, 77, 78, 81, 83, 87, 93, 103, 105, 106
new physics 1, 10, 11, 29, 32, 34n13, 46, 49–51, 54–6, 78, 91, 94, 104

panentheism 52, 64n112, 67
panpsychism 50, 52, 79
patristic tradition 4, 5, 7, 9, 42–4,
  53, 54, 81, 82, 87, 88, 103, 104
predicament of the self 9, 12,
  67–75, 93, 105
Ptolemaic system 3, 4, 9, 12n1

quantum mechanics/physics 8, 11,
  28, 29, 32, 48, 89

reductionism 37, 44, 51, 69, 72, 88,
  91, 93, 95n34
relativity 11, 21, 25, 28, 29, 48
retrieval/return of the self 67, 74–80,
  82, 84, 87, 89, 91, 93, 105

Saints (their experiences and
  perceptions) 46, 55, 56, 66n142,
  81, 83, 85, 88

science-engaged theology 1–12, 35,
  43, 84–6, 90, 92, 103–6
scientific method 7, 9, 35, 39, 41,
  51, 54, 56n1, 57n2, 79, 91–3,
  95n27, 105, 106
sola scriptura 38, 39, 51, 54, 58n20,
  68, 70, 76, 87–9, 105
supernatural (aspect of reality) 10,
  47, 51–6, 74, 80, 83, 93
synergy 10, 41, 52, 64n114, 84

Tabula rasa universe *see sola
  scriptura*
Theory of Everything 11, 28, 32,
  48, 51
transformation (of life/perception/
  the universe) 5, 45, 46, 48,
  55, 56, 61n73, 80, 81, 83–7,
  89, 90

For Product Safety Concerns and Information please contact our EU representative GPSR@taylorandfrancis.com
Taylor & Francis Verlag GmbH, Kaufingerstraße 24, 80331 München, Germany

www.ingramcontent.com/pod-product-compliance
Lightning Source LLC
Chambersburg PA
CBHW071822230426
43670CB00013B/2539